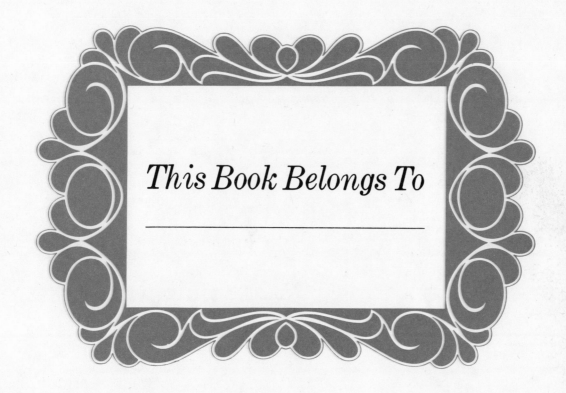

This Book Belongs To

_____

GREAT BIG JOKE & RIDDLE BOOK

GREAT BIG JOKE & RIDDLE BOOK

Compiled and edited by OSCAR WEIGLE
Illustrated by CROSBY BONSALL, JOHN HUEHNERGARTH,
SUSAN PERL, and BILL and BONNIE RUTHERFORD

GROSSET & DUNLAP • Publishers • NEW YORK

Library of Congress Catalog Card Number: 79-129734

The contents of this book were previously published under the following
titles: *Jokes, Riddles, Funny Stories; The Riddle Book; Ask Me Another
Riddle; Tell Me Another Joke;* and *The Joke Book.*

ISBN: 0-448-02584-1 (TRADE EDITION)
ISBN: 0-448-03167-1 (LIBRARY EDITION)

1981 PRINTING

The Business Whirl

BOSS: You can't just come in here and ask for a raise. You must work yourself up.

EMPLOYEE: I did, sir. Look—I'm trembling all over!

BOSS: Did you mail out those circulars?

NEW MAIL CLERK: No, I couldn't find any round envelopes.

Where is the manager's office?

Keep going along this passageway until you come to a sign that says, "No Admittance." Go right through the door and continue till you see the sign that says, "Keep out." Follow that corridor till you see the sign that says, "Silence." Then yell for him.

Don't you think that this company is like one big family?

No — everybody's been pretty friendly, so far.

BOSS: Did you put that note where it would be sure to attract Mr. Klaf's attention when he came in?

OFFICE BOY: Yes — I stuck a pin through it and put it on his chair.

Is he a successful executive?

I should say so! He has two desks — one for each foot!

JO: How long have you been working here?

ANN: Ever since the boss threatened to fire me.

EMPLOYEE: Could I have tomorrow off, so that I can help my wife with the spring housecleaning?

BOSS: I'm afraid not. We're much too busy.

EMPLOYEE: Thank you, sir. I knew I could depend on you.

I've just come from Detroit where I did a tremendous business. How much do you think I sold?

Oh, about half.

Half of what?

Half of what you say.

My boss does bird imitations. I didn't know he was so talented. He watches me like a hawk!

EMPLOYEE: I've been with the company for five years, doing three men's work for one man's pay, and I demand a raise.

BOSS: Out of the question — but I'll tell you what I'll do. Give me the names of the other two men and I'll fire them.

I see where Bill went into the holdup business.

What?

Yeah — he's a suspender salesman.

SECRETARY: There's a bill collector outside, sir.

BOSS: Did you tell him I was out?

SECRETARY: Yes, but he wouldn't believe me.

BOSS: Then I'll have to go and tell him myself.

FOREMAN: Why do you only carry one plank at a time? All the other men carry two.

WORKER: Well, I guess they're just too lazy to make two trips.

What time is it by your watch?

Ten minutes after.

Ten minutes after what?

I don't know. Times got so bad I had to lay off one of the hands.

"She's fast at sending smoke signals, all right, but she makes too many erasures."

DOOR-TO-DOOR SALESMAN: Is the lady of the house in?

MAN: Yes, but she's asleep right now.

DOOR-TO-DOOR SALESMAN: Good! I'm selling alarm clocks. Take one in and see if it won't do the work.

RECEPTIONIST: I'm sorry, but you can't see Mr. Mayer.

CALLER: Is he in conference?

RECEPTIONIST: No, he's busy.

BOSS: Here is your pay for loafing on the job thirty-five hours.

EMPLOYEE: Excuse me, sir—that should be *forty* hours!

EMPLOYEE: I would like to have a raise in pay, sir.

BOSS: But we just put some extra money in your pay envelope last week!

EMPLOYEE: Why doesn't my wife *tell* me these things?

Boss: If Mr. Koehler calls today, tell him I'm out.

Receptionist: Yes, sir.

Boss: And don't let him catch you doing any work, or he won't believe you.

Warden: What are you going to do when you get out of prison?

Prisoner: I think I'll open a jewelry store.

Warden: That's interesting. But won't that take a lot of money?

Prisoner: Well, the way I look at it, burglar tools are an investment.

Did that advertisement you put in the paper yesterday get quick results?

I should say so! I advertised for a night watchman and last night our place was robbed.

Clerk: I cannot live on my salary, sir.

Boss: Well, I'm sorry to hear that. I was just going to promote you to head of the Economy Department.

Are you a clock-watcher?

No. Business is so slow, I watch the calendar.

ON THIS SITE WILL BE CONSTRUCTED THE CITY OF ROME

"Mark my words, it won't be built in a day."

TEXAS TICKLERS

"What superb grapefruit!" exclaimed a visitor to Texas as he passed a citrus grove.

"Oh, our lemons are a little small now," said the Texan nonchalantly. "We've had a bad season, you know."

A little farther down the road the visitor remarked on the size and color of some flowers.

"Just some little ol' weeds," the Texan said modestly.

Finally they came to the Rio Grande.

"Hmm-m," murmured the visitor, "someone's radiator must be leaking!"

TEXAS BOY: Daddy, I think I'd like to take up the study of stars.

TEXAS FATHER: Good idea. I'll buy Hollywood for you.

TEXAN: What does Alaska have that Texas doesn't have more of?

ALASKAN: Size — and modesty!

TEE: What is that you're reading?

HEE: It's an article entitled, "Teenage Millionaire."

TEE: All about some popular singer, I suppose?

HEE: No, it's about a Texas boy who saved his allowance for three weeks!

"There is the Alamo," said the proud Texan to his friend from Boston. "That ruin is where only 136 Texans held off 15,000 of Santa Ana's army for four days. Did you ever have any heroes like that in Massachusetts?"

"Well, I should say we did!" answered the Bostonian. "We had Paul Revere, for example."

"Paul Revere!" snorted the Texan. "Do you mean that fellow who had to ride to get help?"

FIRST TEXAS FARMER: May I borrow your power saw to cut a watermelon?

SECOND TEXAS FARMER: I'll give it to you as soon as I finish cutting through this cucumber!

A check was once returned to a wealthy Texas oilman from a bank. It was stamped "Insufficient Funds" on the back. Beneath the stamped imprint was a notation from the bank in ink. It read, "Not you — US!"

TEXAS WIFE: The brakes on the car weren't working today, and before I could stop I had run into ten other cars.

TEXAS HUSBAND: My goodness! Where did that happen?

TEXAS WIFE: In our garage.

FIRST FISHERMAN: I once caught an eight-inch fish.

SECOND FISHERMAN: That's nothing special. I've caught many fish that were over *twenty* inches long.

FIRST FISHERMAN: Well, where I come from, we measure our fish between the eyes!

NEW YORKER: The Empire State Building is named after our state. It's really *some* building, isn't it?

TEXAN: It sure is. But it's too bad it was never finished!

Does Tex have a large bankroll? Large? He has to have it put on microfilm before he can get it into his wallet!

A wealthy Texan sauntered into an art gallery during a trip to Europe, selected several paintings by Van Gogh and Rembrandt, and paid for them on the spot.

The art dealer was quite overwhelmed. "Where shall I have these delivered?" he asked.

"Oh, I'll take them with me," said the Texan. "I promised the folks back home I'd send them some cards."

The wealthy Texan was showing his new estate to his friends. "You will observe," he said proudly, "that I have three swimming pools."

"I noticed that," said a friend. "But why so many?"

"Well," said the Texan, "the first pool is filled with cold water and is for the use of my friends who enjoy a cool dip. The second pool is filled with warm water and is for the use of my friends who like to go swimming in warm water."

"And how about the third pool?" asked the friend. "I notice that it has no water in it at all."

"Ah, yes," said the Texan. "That pool is for the use of my friends who can't swim!"

RICK: Is it true that that rich man has four Cadillacs?

ROCK: Yes — one for each direction.

The Texas millionaire walked into the Cadillac salesroom. "My wife has a touch of flu," he told the salesman. "Do you have anything in the way of a get-well car?"

Tex is one of the poorer cowboys. How so?

He only has a one-horse garage.

VISITOR: Do you have many Chinese restaurants in Texas?

TEXAN: Why, yes, of course. And let me tell you — they have *real* fortune cookies. When you break them open, you'll find a $100 bill!

PUN-ishment

After many years of special training, a dog was able to play tunes on a piano. And after still more years the animal was able to play a complete Bach sonata.

People came from near and far to see and hear this amazing demonstration. But when one of the onlookers had a coughing spell during the dog's featured piano recital, the dog stopped playing at once, growled, and bared its teeth at the offender.

It was then that the dog's trainer came to the rescue. "Don't worry," he told the cowering man. "His Bach is worse than his bite."

Is there a lot of money to be made in the cattle business?

Well, so I've herd.

HUNTER: I once shot a lion fifteen feet long.

SKEPTIC: Some lyin'!

That girl is a peach.

You mean she's sweet?

No, she has a heart of stone.

Did you ever try to tickle a mule?

No. Why?

You'd get a big kick out of it!

". . . and now for the latest gnus."

TEACHER: Can you use the word "mutilate" in a sentence, please.

JOHNNY: Daddy would like our cat better if she didn't mutilate at night.

KEVIN: What will you have to drink?

MYLES: Ginger ale.

KEVIN: Pale?

MYLES: Oh, no — just a glass, please.

When rain falls, does it ever get up again?

Oh, yes — in dew time.

BRITISH CAMPER: What's that?

AMERICAN CAMPER: It's just an owl.

BRITISH CAMPER: Quite so, but who's 'owling?

FIRST LION: Well, I'm going into the arena soon.

SECOND LION: Yes, we're here to-day and gone to martyr.

MARTY: Gee, I can't make up my mind whether I should ask Kate or Edith to be my wife.

SMARTY: Well, you can't have your Kate and Edith, too!

PINKY: How did the bullfight come out?

Dinky: Oh, it was a toss-up.

LENNY: I just love to be in the country and hear the trees whisper.

DENNY: Yes, but I hate to hear the grass mown.

Did anyone laugh when the fat lady fell on the ice?

No, but the ice made some awful cracks!

When I want to watch a late show on television, I set my clock back an hour.

What for?

I call it Delight Saving Time.

FLO: I have a run in my stocking. It started yesterday.

FRAN: Really, dear, you shouldn't wear stockings two days running.

BOBBY: I'll bet you a quarter that I've got the hardest name in the world.

BILLY: All right. What's your name?

BOBBY: Stone!

BILLY: Pay me the quarter. My name is Harder.

FIRST JAILBREAKER: How did you get rid of the bloodhounds that were trailing us?

SECOND JAILBREAKER: I threw a penny in the stream and they followed the cent.

ANIMAL FARE

The father polar bear, the mother polar bear and the baby polar bear were all sitting on an iceberg in the Arctic Ocean.

"I've got a tale to tell," said the father polar bear.

"And *I've* got a tale to tell, too," said the mother polar bear.

Just then the baby polar bear stood up. "My tail," he said, "is told."

Isn't that little thing too small to be a watchdog?

No. He's a wrist watchdog.

HOST: Come right into the house. Don't mind the dog.

VISITOR: Doesn't he bite?

HOST: That's what I want to find out. I just bought him this morning.

TEE: What would you do if you saw a bear?

HEE: I'd climb a tree.

TEE: But don't you know that bears can climb trees, too?

HEE: Well, I know that, but my tree would be shaking too much!

FIRST HUNTER: Shoot, quick! Hit that lion!

SECOND HUNTER: But I can't. This is an elephant gun.

EXPLORER: I was once stranded on an island and on the verge of starvation. I eventually became so hungry that I dined off my pet parrot.

LISTENER: What did it taste like?

EXPLORER: Oh, turkey, chicken, wild duck, goose — that parrot could imitate anything!

MRS. FEE: Pardon me for asking, but why are there three round holes near the bottom of your back door?

MRS. LINE: Oh, those holes are for my three cats — they can go outdoors any time at all without my having to open the door for them.

MRS. FEE: But wouldn't one hole do just as well?

MRS. LINE: No. When I say "Scat!" I *mean* "Scat!"

What do raccoons eat?
What they can find.
And if they can't find anything?
They eat something else.

SPECTATOR: I wonder what that tiger would say if it could speak.

ZOOKEEPER: It would probably say, "Pardon me, sir, but I'm a leopard."

This dog must be a good watchdog.
How do you know?
He's so full of ticks!

SMALL BOY: Why does the giraffe have such a long neck?

ZOOKEEPER: Well, you see, the giraffe's head is so far removed from his body that a long neck is absolutely necessary.

"What an odd-looking carpet that is under the elephant!" remarked the visitor to the circus.

"Oh, that's no carpet," corrected the elephant's keeper. "That's the man who offered the elephant some chewing tobacco."

WOMAN: Why are all the monkeys out of their cages?

ZOOKEEPER: It's a holiday. This is Charles Darwin's birthday.

HUNTER: The trees grow so closely together in the jungle that you can't even shove your hand between the trunks. And as for game, I've seen deer with a ten-foot spread of antlers!

LISTENER: But how can the deer get those antlers between those tree trunks?

HUNTER: That is *their* problem!

FIRST RACE HORSE: Don't you remember me?

SECOND RACE HORSE: The pace is familiar, but I don't remember the mane.

Say, your puppy just bit me on the ankle!

Well, you wouldn't expect a little dog to bite your neck, would you?

This is a baseball dog.

What's that?

Well, he wears a muzzle, catches flies, chases fowls and beats it for home when he sees the catcher.

EXPLORER: I would enjoy going into that lagoon for a swim. Are you sure there are no crocodiles about?

NATIVE: Very sure. The sharks have scared them all away!

A man walked into an ice-cream parlor with two large sheep dogs one day and asked for three super-special ice cream sundaes. The man behind the counter was somewhat taken aback, but he dutifully prepared the ice cream sundaes and served them to the man and his dogs. All three of them ate the sundaes with obvious enjoyment. Then the man paid the bill and all three of them left.

The very next day the two sheep dogs came into the ice-cream parlor all by themselves. They hopped up onto some stools, put their paws on the counter, and otherwise made it apparent that they would like to be served. The man behind the counter smiled understandingly, shrugged his shoulders, and then prepared a couple of super-specials, which he promptly put before the two sheep dogs. Again the dogs ate up every last bit of the sundaes and then left.

Shortly afterward the owner of the sheep dogs came into the ice-cream parlor. "That was an exceptionally kind thing you did for my two dogs a while ago," he began, "and I want you to know that I'm very grateful."

"Not at all," said the counterman with a wave of his hand. "After all, I couldn't help but remember them from yesterday, and since they enjoyed the sundaes so much, I was glad to oblige."

"Nevertheless," said the dog owner, "I want to express my appreciation in a more material way. I would like to give you this magnificent lobster." So saying, he handed over to the counterman a large live lobster.

"But — but — " stammered the counterman, "you really shouldn't have done this. However, it is a magnificent lobster. If you insist, I'll take him home to my wife and we'll have him for dinner."

"Well," said the dog owner, "he's already had dinner. But I think he might enjoy going to a movie!"

"...and they lived hoppily ever after."

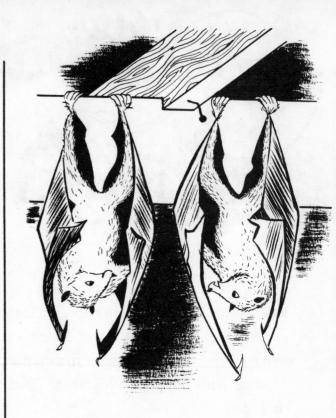

"I suppose we should be thankful that we've got a roof over our head."

"Don't be a nag!"

"You'll never get me up in one of those things."

Classroom Capers

TEACHER: Are the examination questions giving you any trouble?

PUPIL: No. The questions are clear. It's the answers.

STUDENT: I don't think I should get a zero on this examination paper!

TEACHER: Neither do I, but that's the lowest mark there is.

TEACHER: Bobby, please spell "new."

BOBBY: N-e-w.

TEACHER: Very good. Now spell "canoe."

BOBBY: K-n-e-w.

TEACHER: Name a collective noun.

PUPIL: Garbage truck.

STUDENT: Excuse me, but I can't see when you are between me and the blackboard.

TEACHER: I do my best to make myself clear, but I can't make myself transparent.

What marks did you get last term in Physical Education?

I didn't get any marks — only a few bruises.

TEACHER: As we have just learned, the earth is round and hangs in space without any support. Oliver, please tell the class how you can prove it.

OLIVER: I don't have to prove it. I never said that it does!

TEACHER: What great event occurred in 1492?

PUPIL: Columbus discovered America.

TEACHER: Correct. And what happened in 1500?

PUPIL: Hmm-m ... America had its eighth birthday?

Name six animals of the arctic regions.

Three walruses and three polar bears.

TEACHER: What is the principal river of Egypt?

PUPIL: The Nile.

TEACHER: Correct. Can you tell me the names of some of its smaller tributaries?

PUPIL: The juve-niles, I think.

TEACHER: When water becomes ice, what is the greatest change that takes place?

STUDENT: The price.

TEACHER: For what is Switzerland famous?

STUDENT: Swiss cheese.

TEACHER: Oh, can't you think of something grander — more impressive?

STUDENT: Limburger?

"Can anyone tell me what these Roman numerals stand for?" the teacher asked her class as she wrote on the blackboard: LXXX.

Mary Smith raised her hand. "I know," she said. "It's 'Love and kisses.'"

SCHOOL SUPERINTENDENT: Are there any unusual children in your class?

TEACHER: Yes — three of them have good manners.

TEACHER: Why are you shivering, Peter?

PETER: I guess it must be this zero on my test paper.

TOMMY: The teacher says I'm very good at arithmetic, Daddy.

FATHER: Really? Well, let me test you. How much is one and one?

TOMMY: We haven't gotten that far, yet.

TEACHER: Can you give a me an example of an imaginary spheroid?
STUDENT: Yes — a rooster's egg.

SCIENCE TEACHER: The light of the sun travels to us at a rate of about 186,000 miles a second.
STUDENT: Yes, but it's all downhill!

TEACHER: Now, class, are there any questions?
PUPIL: Yes. Where do those words go when you rub them off the blackboard?

The classroom period seemed to be a dismal failure. As each pupil was called up by the teacher to answer a question on the subject under discussion, the answer was always either incorrect or "I don't know."

Finally the bell rang, signaling the end of the period. "Class is dismissed," sighed the teacher wearily, "and please don't flap your ears on the way out."

Daffynitions

ADVICE: Something you give when you're too old to act yourself.

ALARM CLOCK: Something to scare the daylight into you.

ASTRONAUT: Someone who takes over when the chimps are down.

BABY SITTER: Someone who takes hush money.

BASEBALL BAT: A fly swatter.

BERET: A hat that keeps an artist's hair out of his paint.

BUDGET: A system of worrying before you spend, as well as later.

CANNIBAL: Something that can be in cans.

CATERPILLAR: A worm wearing a sweater.

COMMITTEE: A group that keeps minutes and wastes hours.

DOG SHOW: Oodles of poodles.

EGOTIST: Someone who is always me-deep in conversation.

EIFFEL TOWER: The Empire State Building, after taxes.

FORGER: A man who is always ready to write a wrong.

FREE FLIGHT: What airline employees get.

GROWNUP: Someone who has stopped growing at both ends and started growing in the middle.

HOME: Where part of the family waits until the others are through with the car.

HYPODERMIC NEEDLE: A sick shooter.

IDEAL: My turn to shuffle.

I. O. U.: A paper wait.

JUNK PILE: A goat's restaurant.

KNUCKLE: Five pennies.

LAWSUIT: A policeman's uniform.

LEGEND: A lie that has attained the dignity of age.

LIVER: A long rod for lifting heavy weights.

LUCK: The other person's formula.

MISCHIEF: The Chief's daughter.

MOUNTAIN CLIMBER: Someone who wants to take another peak.

MOUTH: The grocer's friend, the dentist's fortune, the speaker's pride, and the fool's trap.

OLD-TIMER: One who remembers when scientists taught that everything that goes up must come down.

QUADRUPLETS: Four crying out loud.

SEWING CIRCLE: A place where women go to needle each other.

SHOPPER: Someone who likes to go buy-buy.

SPACE STATION: A parking garage.

SPANKING: Stern punishment.

SURGEON: Rushing forward.

SWISS CHEESE: A bunch of holes strung together.

TENT CATERPILLAR: A worm who likes to camp out.

Sillier and Sillier

A silly got into a taxicab. "Drive around the park twenty times," he directed the driver.

The taxi driver did as he was told. The tenth time around, the passenger tapped the driver on the shoulder.

"Faster!" he shouted. "I'm in a hurry!"

Say, who do you think you're pushing?

How many guesses do I get?

KERRY: What do they do with doughnut holes?

TERRY: They use them to stuff macaroni.

What is the capital of Delaware?
Trenton, New Jersey.
Thanks. I thought so.

DRIVING INSTRUCTOR: Hey, what are you doing? Put down that gun!

STUDENT: Well, you told me to kill the motor!

I keep thinking that today is Monday.

Well, today *is* Monday.

I know. That's why I keep thinking it is.

MAN: Have you got any mail for me?

MAILMAN: What's your name?

MAN: You'll find it on the envelope.

I got up at dawn yesterday to see the sun rise.

Well, you couldn't have picked a better time!

SILLY: For years I've been cheating myself at solitaire.

BILLY: Don't you ever catch yourself cheating?

SILLY: No, I'm too clever.

I always do my hardest work before breakfast.

What is that?

Getting up.

HOPE: Ouch! That water burned my hand!

DOPE: You should have felt it before you put your hand in it.

How do you like your new watch?

Terrific! If I wind it up tight enough, it does an hour in fifty-five minutes!

I'm a dairy maid in a candy factory.

What do you do?

I milk chocolates.

Why do you think this fellow is silly?

Well, you know that poster in the post office that says, "Man Wanted for Robbery in Philadelphia"?

Yes.

Well, he went in and applied for the job.

TEACHER: Spell "cattle."

JIMMY: C-a-t-t-t-l-e.

TEACHER: Leave out one of those t's.

JIMMY: Which one?

I once dropped my watch out of a third-story window onto a concrete pavement — and it ran for days without stopping.

It must have been pretty scared!

May I have some more orange juice?

Take it easy — oranges don't grow on trees, you know.

"We're having fish for dinner!"

Excuse me for living.

All right, but don't let it happen again.

MRS. SILL: All the clocks in the house have run down, dear. Why don't you go into town and find out what time it is?

MR. SILL: I haven't got a watch. You'll have to lend me one.

MRS. SILL: Watch? You won't need a watch. Just write it down on a piece of paper.

Is there anything at all you're sure of?

I'm sure I don't know.

Have you got something in your eye?

No, I'm just trying to look through my finger.

WARDEN: I'm going to put you on bread and water as punishment. How do you like it?

CONVICT: Whole wheat—toasted.

IRA: That's a sick-looking watch you have there.

MARTIN: Yes, its hours are numbered.

I invented spaghetti.

Where did you get the idea?

From my noodle.

What's your name?

Oh, it's a French name.

Well, what is it?

I can't say. I don't speak French.

Arthur, you have your shoes on the wrong feet.

But they're the only feet I have!

Did you take a cold bath this morning?

No. There wasn't any hot water.

HERMAN: For some time now I have been weighing myself on those scales that hand out cards. When I started, I weighed 135 pounds. Now I weigh 190 pounds.

SHERMAN: How is it that you've gained so much?

HERMAN: My pockets are full of those cards!

Do you hear something?

No.

That's funny. I'm talking to you.

WOMAN: Say, that chicken I bought from you the other day had no wishbone.

BUTCHER: Yes, well — you see, the chickens we get are so happy, they have nothing further to wish for!

I was running down the street when something fell on my head.

What fell on your head?

Me.

Robert Burns wrote "To a Field Mouse."

Did he get an answer?

POST OFFICE CLERK: Is this package for you? The name is obliterated.

MAN: No, that can't be mine. My name is O'Brien.

KIM: Your alarm clock was ringing about an hour ago.

PIM: Well, why didn't you tell me then?

KIM: You were asleep!

What's the date today?

You have a newspaper in your pocket. Look at it.

Yes, but it's yesterday's paper.

JIMMY: Mom, can I watch the eclipse?

MOTHER: Oh, all right—but don't get too close!

Say, this boat leaks!

Only at one end. We'll just sit at the other end.

PAUL: I once had to live on a can of beans for a whole week.

MIKE: My goodness! Weren't you afraid of falling off?

"Will you marry me?"
"I'm your other end, silly!"

This boat doesn't have a fo'castle.
Well, I'll give you two two-castles.

I think it's going to rain before evening.

Oh, I hope not. I want to water my garden.

JOHNNY: Our English teacher doesn't know what he's talking about.

JIM: What makes you say that?

JOHNNY: He's never been to England.

I would like to apply for some fire insurance.

Certainly. For your home, sir?

No, it's for me. Every time I get a new job, I get fired!

A woman went into a butcher shop and asked the proprietor, "Do you have any beef kidleys?"

"I suppose you mean *kidneys,*" said the butcher.

"Well," said the woman, "that's what I saidle, diddle I?"

BARRY: Are you going to the masquerade party?

HARRY: Yes.

BARRY: Why are you wearing two suits?

HARRY: I'm going as twins.

Is this a second-hand store?
Yes.
Well, I want one for my watch.

Counter Quips

CUSTOMER: These shoes are much too narrow and pointed.

SHOE CLERK: That's what they're wearing this season.

CUSTOMER: Perhaps so, but I'm still wearing last season's feet.

CUSTOMER: Are you quite sure that these binoculars are high-powered ones?

CLERK: I should say so! When you use these binoculars, anything less than ten miles away looks as if it were behind you!

CUSTOMER: The first time I put on this coat and buttoned it up, I burst the seam down the back!

TAILOR: That just shows how well our buttons are sewed on, sir.

CUSTOMER (with laryngitis): What ice cream flavors do you have?

SODA FOUNTAIN CLERK (whispering): Chocolate, vanilla and strawberry.

CUSTOMER: Say — do you have laryngitis, too?

SODA FOUNTAIN CLERK: No, only chocolate, vanilla and strawberry!

CUSTOMER: Have you anything for gray hair?

SALES CLERK: Nothing but the greatest respect, sir.

CUSTOMER: Do you have a good used television set for sale?

DEALER: Yes, sir. Here's a set that's hardly ever been used. It belonged to an old lady with weak eyes.

CUSTOMER (in drug store): Do you have mustard plasters?

SALES CLERK: We're all out of mustard, ma'am. How about mayonnaise?

SALES CLERK: This hat, madam, is the best hat in the shop.

LADY CUSTOMER: I know it is, but I'd like a change. That's my hat.

CUSTOMER: I can't find words to express my annoyance with you!

SALES CLERK: May I sell you a dictionary, sir?

MRS. HOMEBODY: I sent my little boy to your store for two pounds of grapes and you only sent me a pound and a half. Something must be wrong with your scales.

STOREKEEPER: My scales are all right, Mrs. Homebody. Have you weighed your little boy?

CUSTOMER: Those ivory carvings you sold me last week turned out to be imitation.

CLERK: I just can't understand that — unless the elephant had a false tooth.

TEENAGER (in music store): I'm looking for a song that goes Umpity-Bumpity-Zoom-Zoom-Zam.

SALES CLERK: What are the words?

TEENAGER: *Those* are the words, silly!

CUSTOMER: What's good for my wife's fallen arches?

SHOE SALESMAN: Rubber heels.

CUSTOMER: With what?

SHOPPER: Don't you think that these eggs are rather small?

STOREKEEPER: Yes, I do. That's the trouble with the farmers. They're so anxious to sell their eggs, they take them out of the nests too soon!

CUSTOMER: Do you keep stationery?

CLERK: Up to a certain point — then I go all to pieces.

NEW FATHER: How much are those diapers?

SALES CLERK: One dollar — and three cents for tax.

NEW FATHER: Oh, well, we've been using safety pins.

GOOD FOR WHAT AILS YOU

DOCTOR: The check you gave me last week came back.

PATIENT: So did the pain in my chest.

MOTHER: Doctor, how is my little boy — the one who swallowed the half dollar?

DOCTOR: I don't see any change yet.

Is it true, doctor, that women live longer than men?

Yes, especially widows.

NERVE SPECIALIST: I can cure you for $2,000.

PATIENT: Will mine ever be as good as yours?

DOCTOR: Did you open both windows in your bedroom last night, as I told you to do?

PATIENT: Well, I only have one window in my room, doctor, so I opened it twice.

My doctor says I can't play tennis. Ah, so he's played with you, too?

WOMAN: Will my false teeth look natural?

DENTIST: I make them so natural, they ache!

Imagine meeting you here at the psychiatrist's office! Are you coming or going?

If I knew that, I wouldn't be here!

DOCTOR: Thanks to me, you're another man.

PATIENT: Right! And please send your bill to the other man.

That fellow over there is handicapped with an eye disorder. Everything he looks at, he sees double.

Poor man! I imagine he must find it hard to get a job.

No. The gas and electric company hired him to read meters.

PATIENT: Doctor, you must do something for me. I snore so loudly, I wake myself up.

DOCTOR: In that case, I would advise you to sleep in another room.

WOMAN: You promised my husband that you would save his life, but he died this morning.

DOCTOR: I'm sorry to hear that, but perhaps he didn't follow my instructions.

WOMAN: Yes, he did. He took your medicine for a month.

DOCTOR: Well, there you are! I told him to take it for two months!

DOCTOR: What is your name?

PATIENT: Abraham Lincoln.

DOCTOR: *Abraham Lincoln?* Well, what can I do for you?

PATIENT: I think my wife is trying to get rid of me. She keeps insisting that I take her to the theater.

"Dr. Fletcher's office — who's coughing?"

OFFICE HOURS
MON......9 - 4
TUES.......9 - 4
WED......12 - 4
THURS....9 - 7
FRI........9 - 4

FAMILY FROLICS

Mom, I just knocked down the ladder that was standing up against the side of the house.

Go and tell your father.

He knows all about it. He's hanging onto the roof!

BILLY: I wonder why the man next door is always buying dishes.

TILLIE: He's probably married to a smashing young thing.

DEBBIE: My ancestors came over on the Mayflower.

BETTY: My ancestors came over a month before — on the April Shower.

WIFE: Do you think we ought to have butterfly chairs?

HUSBAND: No, let them stand up or fly around.

HOUSEWIFE: If you will come in the house, I'll give you a good meal. Are your feet dirty?

TRAMP: Yes, they are, ma'am, but don't worry — I've got my shoes on!

Who is your wife going to vote for — a Democrat or a Republican?

She'll vote for the man I vote for.

And who are you going to vote for?

She hasn't decided yet.

My wife doesn't understand me at all. Does yours?

Really, old chap, I don't believe she's ever met you!

MR. WOOD: How is Mrs. Stone and all the little pebbles?

MR. STONE: Fine, thank you. And how is Mrs. Wood and all the little splinters?

MOTHER: You didn't set a place at the table for your little brother, Susie.

SUSIE: I don't have to. He eats like a horse.

I wish that my wife would get a few new recipes.

Why? What's the matter with the ones she has now?

Well, for one thing, they all start out the same way — "defrost!"

Why is Harry pacing the floor like that?

Well, he's terribly worried about his wife.

Really? What does she have?
His new car.

MRS. JONES: My goodness, Fred, this isn't our baby! This is the wrong baby carriage!

MR. JONES: Sh-h! This is a better baby carriage!

My husband has an absolutely even temper.

Always good?

No. Always terrible!

MR. DEIGH: So today is your silver wedding anniversary?

MR. KNIGHT: Yes — and that's the first twenty-five years of it out of the way.

My people were one of the first families of Virginia.

And mine were one of the oiliest in Oklahoma.

HUSBAND: I just took out another ten thousand dollar life insurance policy today.

WIFE: Oh, I could kill you!

Mr. Wilson, I'm afraid your son is going to the dogs.

No, he's too lazy. The dogs are going to have to come to him.

WIFE: My mother won't stay in this house another day unless we get rid of the mice.

HUSBAND: Excuse me.

WIFE: Where are you going?

HUSBAND: To get rid of the cat.

The baby twins had just been brought to the church for the christening. "What are their names?" asked the minister.

"Steak and Kidney," answered the father.

"Don't mind my husband," said the mother hurriedly. "He's a little excited. He means Kate and Sidney."

MRS. PEPPER: I understand your husband can speak six languages.

MRS. POPPER: Yes, and I can tell him to wash the dishes in all of them!

JENKINS: I understand that your wife always counts to ten when she's angry.

JONES: Yes, but it's usually over me!

Is your wife influenced by articles in newspapers and magazines?

She must be. This week, every time I asked her to do something for me, she said, "Do it yourself!"

WIFE: How do you like my new dress?

HUSBAND: Like three months' salary.

My wife writes me that she is all unstrung. What shall I do?

Send her a wire.

"Don't you think we ought to get another umbrella, dear?"

RUFUS: Your wife has fallen into the well.

GOOFUS: Oh, that's all right — we use city water now.

What does your wife do with empty soda bottles?

She breaks them over my head.

MOTHER: Charlotte, where is your little sister?

CHARLOTTE: In the next room, Mother.

MOTHER: Well, go see what she's doing and tell her to stop it!

JERRY: Why is Daddy singing to the baby tonight?

MOTHER: He's trying to sing him to sleep.

JERRY: If I was the baby, I'd pretend I was asleep.

MOTHER: I have just discovered a way to get Richard up in the morning. I just open the door to his room and throw the cat on his bed.

FATHER: How does that wake him up?

MOTHER: Well, the dog sleeps on his bed, too.

TIM: This is a picture of my great-great-grandfather.

TOM: Why, he doesn't look any older than you!

I saw your wife yesterday.

What did she have to say?

Oh, nothing. Why?

Then it couldn't have been my wife!

HUSBAND: I've just insured my life for thirty thousand dollars, so that if anything happens to me, you and the children will be provided for.

WIFE: How thoughtful of you! Now you won't have to go and see the doctor every time you feel sick, will you?

Is your wife as beautiful these days as she was when I last saw her?

Yes, but now it takes her a little longer.

HUSBAND: That button is still off my shirt.

WIFE: Yes, dear — I'm saving on thread.

Mirth on the Menu

DINER: Have you any wild duck?

WAITER: No, sir, but we can take a tame one and irritate him for you.

Waiter, what is this?

Scotch Rarebit, sir.

And what is Scotch Rarebit?

A Welsh Rarebit with less cheese.

WAITRESS: We're proud of our service and our food. If you order a fresh egg, you'll be served the freshest egg in the world. Order crisp bacon and you'll get the crispest bacon in the world. Order black coffee and you'll get the blackest coffee in the world.

DINER: What you say must be true. I ordered a small steak.

WAITER: I couldn't help but notice, sir, that you brushed off your plate before you were served.

DINER: It's just a habit, I'm afraid. I'm a baseball umpire.

I would like a cup of coffee and a muttered buffin.

You mean a buffered muttin, don't you?

No, I mean a muffered buttin.

Wouldn't you like some doughnuts and milk?

DINER: I've heard that fish is brain food, but I don't care for it. Isn't there some other kind of brain food?

WAITRESS: Well, there's always noodle soup.

Why are you washing your fork in the finger bowl?

I don't want to get my pocket dirty.

NIT: There's a lot of juice in this grapefruit.

WIT: Yes — more than meets the eye.

DINER: May I have the check, please?

WAITER: What did you have, sir?

DINER: Let's see . . . there were three fish —

WAITER: I only brought you two, I believe.

DINER: No, there were three. I had two haddock — and one smelt!

DINER: What is your special to-day?

WAITRESS: What we couldn't get rid of yesterday.

Waiter, haven't you forgotten me? No — you're the flounder.

DINER: This doesn't look or taste much like chicken soup.

WAITER: Well, it's chicken soup in its infancy, sir. It's made out of the water the eggs were boiled in.

Waiter, I don't like the looks of this trout.

If it's looks you want, why don't you order some goldfish?

HOSTESS: It's beginning to rain. You'll get wet. Maybe you'd better stay to dinner.

GUEST: Oh, no — it's not raining as badly as that!

DINER: Do you think lobsters are healthy?

WAITER: I think so. I've never heard one complain.

DINER: Waiter, this sauerkraut isn't sour enough.

WAITER: But, sir — that isn't sauerkraut. That's noodles!

DINER: Oh! Well, for noodles it's much *too* sour!

Can you eat two desserts at once? Yes, immediately!

Smile When You Say That!

BEN: It's a funny thing — all dogs, no matter how vicious, will come up to me and lick my hand.

KEN: Maybe if you'd eat with a knife and fork, they wouldn't be so friendly.

I play entirely by ear.
You ought to remember that people listen the same way.

TED: What a terrible voice! Do you know who that singer is?

FRED: Yes. She's my wife.

TED: Oh, I beg your pardon. Of course, it isn't her voice, really — it's the stuff she has to sing. I wonder who wrote that awful song.

FRED: I did.

CUSTOMER: I refuse to accept these pictures! Why, my husband looks like a chimpanzee!

PHOTOGRAPHER: I can't help it, madam. You picked him. I didn't.

Why do Margie and Harry hate you so much?
I once told them they looked alike.

DEE: This is going to be a real battle of wits.

BATES: How brave of you to fight unarmed!

I'll bet I can make a worse face than you can.
You ought to be able to do that. Look at what you've got to start with!

CHIC: When I read of all the marvels of science, it certainly makes me stop and think.

DICK: Well, well, isn't it wonderful what science can do!

You've heard of faces that stop clocks?

Yes.

Hers stops calendars.

Don't you think that that soprano has a perfectly heavenly voice?

Well, I wouldn't go so far as to say that — but it *is* unearthly.

When one is an actor, one must be able to turn one's personality on and off, like a faucet.

You must have a leaky washer — all I hear is a drip.

MRS. WALKER: Please don't bring your dog into the house. It's full of fleas.

MRS. TALKER: Well, all right, but I never would have thought you'd let your house get into such a condition!

"Only caught one fish, eh?"

Going Places

ELDERLY LADY: What's that up there?

SAILOR: That's the crow's nest, ma'am.

ELDERLY LADY: Oh, really? Could I just peek at the little darlings?

I understand you were in Venice not too long ago.

Yes — it's a wonderful place.

Did you see the gondolas?

Yes, I had dinner with them.

HUSBAND: Good news! I've saved enough money so we can go to Europe this summer.

WIFE: Wonderful! When are we leaving?

HUSBAND: As soon as I've saved enough money for us to come back.

TOURIST: I once visited a castle and saw a bed twenty feet long.

FRIEND: That sounds like a lot of bunk to me.

What is the cheapest way to get to New Orleans?

Arrange to be born there.

SLIM: What are you going to do on your vacation?

JIM: I'm going on a Roman holiday.

SLIM: What's that?

JIM: I'll go Roman around the country.

Mr. Blodgett tells some wonderful stories. He must be a great traveler.

No, but his mind wanders a lot.

NORTHERN ESKIMO: Glub, glub, glub.

SOUTHERN ESKIMO: Glub, glub, glub, you all.

I can now speak Spanish as well as I speak English.

But you mispronounce many words.

Well, I mispronounce lots of English words, too.

HARRY: Did George see much poverty in Europe?

NANCY: Yes — and he brought some of it home with him!

TOURIST: You mean to tell me that you've lived in this out-of-the-way town for more than twenty-five years? I can't see what there is here to keep you busy.

NATIVE: There isn't anything to keep me busy. That's why I like it!

I come from South Dakota.

That's funny — you don't talk like a Southerner.

PHINEAS: In Hawaii they have the same weather all year 'round.

PHOGG: Really? How do people start their conversations?

FATHER: What station did the conductor just call out?

SON: He didn't call out any station, Dad. He just sneezed.

FATHER: Get your things. We must be coming into Kalamazoo.

SY: Are you enjoying the ocean?

HY: No, it bores me. When you've seen one wave, you've seen them all.

I spent last winter in a very pretty city in Switzerland.

Berne?

No, I nearly froze.

An airplane containing the pilot and his only passenger were circling high above a small playing field. Suddenly the pilot cut his motor and began gliding.

"Do you know what?" chuckled the pilot as he looked down. "I'll bet half of the people down there right now think we're going to crash."

The passenger gulped nervously. "Half of us up here do, too," he said weakly.

'PUN MY WORD!

Say, did you read in the newspaper about the fellow who ate six dozen pancakes at one sitting?
No, how waffle!

Do you like your job, cleaning chimneys?
Soots me!

If you were locked in a room with nothing but a calendar and a bed, what would you eat and drink?
Eat the dates on the calendar and drink from the springs on the bed!

How much of that Swiss cheese did you eat?
The whole of it.

A Russian named Rudolph looked out of the window one morning and announced, "It's raining."
His wife looked out also and then said, "No, it's sleeting."
"It's raining," insisted the husband. "Rudolph the Red knows rain, dear!"

Reverend Martin and Reverend Gardner had a long telephone conversation this morning.
Hmm-m-m. Parson to parson, no doubt!

Why are telephone rates quite high in Iran?
Because everyone there speaks Persian to Persian.

I work in a candle company as a trimmer on Saturdays and Sundays.
Don't you work there the rest of the week?
No — just on wick ends.

Was your sister angry when she tried to get away from the skunk?
Not angry — but terribly incensed.

That suit fits you like a bandage.
Yes, I bought it by accident.

I think the library is on fire.
How can you tell it's the library?
I see volumes of smoke.

This suit is getting frayed.
'Fraid of what?

Where's the English channel?
It's not on *my* TV set!

There's the Dog Star.
Are you Sirius?

What did the beaver say to the tree?
It's been nice gnawing you.

Have you read "Freckles"?
No, just plain old brown ones.

I understand that your wife likes to talk.
Yes, she's been that way ever since she went home to mutter.

Do you think that if I wash, my face will be clean?
Let's soap for the best.

Why are you always so friendly with waitresses?
I play for large steaks.

Why does that letter bring tears to your eyes?
It's written on onion skin.

How did you know you needed a shave?
A little beard told me!

Baby candle: Mama, I feel hot.
Mama candle: Hush, dear, it's only glowing pains.

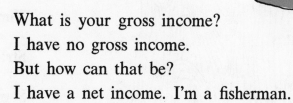

What is your gross income?
I have no gross income.
But how can that be?
I have a net income. I'm a fisherman.

What are taxes?
Little nails.

Why don't you shoo the flies?
Aaa-a, let 'em go barefoot!

What did the pencil say to the paper?
I dot my eyes on you!

Did you hear about the worm who joined the Army?
No.
He's in the apple corps.

Don't you know that everybody loves a fat man?
Yes, but they make up jokes at his expanse.

Is this a real Hawaiian band?
No, but everyone thinks it is because it plays everything in wacky-key.

TONGUE TWISTERS

A skunk sat on a stump.
The stump thunk the skunk stunk.
The skunk thunk the stump stunk.

Cross crossings cautiously.

Six snakes, slipping and sliding.

Bisquick — kiss quick.

Tim, the thin twin tinsmith.

Strange strategic statistics.

She sells sea shells by the seashore.

The sun shines on the shop signs.

She stood at the door of Mrs. Smith's fish-sauce shop, welcoming him in.

Peter Piper picked a peck of pickled peppers.
Did Peter Piper pick a peck of pickled peppers?
If Peter Piper picked a peck of pickled peppers, where's the peck of
    pickled peppers Peter Piper picked?

Theophilus Thistle, the successful thistle-sifter,
While sifting a sieve full of unsifted thistles,
Thrust three thousand thistles through the thick of his thumb.
Now, if Theophilus Thistle, while sifting a sieve full of unsifted thistles,
Thrust three thousand thistles through the thick of his thumb,
See that thou, while sifting a sieve full of unsifted thistles,
Thrust not three thousand thistles through the thick of thy thumb!
(Success to the successful thistle-sifter!)

THE BUTTER BETTY BOUGHT

Betty Botta bought some butter.
"But," said she, "this butter's bitter!
If I put it in my batter,
It will make my batter bitter.
But a bit o' better butter
Will but make my batter better."
So she bought a bit o' butter
Better than the bitter butter,
Made her bitter batter better.
So 'twas better Betty Botta
Bought a bit o' better butter.

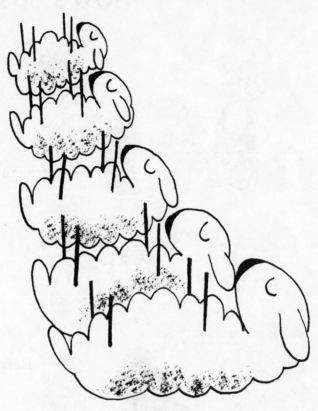

Sheep shouldn't sleep in a shack.
Sheep should sleep in a shed.

If a Hottentot tot taught a Hottentot tot to talk e'er the tot could totter, ought the Hottentot tot be taught to say aught, or naught, or what ought to be taught her?

If to hoot and to toot a Hottentot tot be taught by a Hottentot tutor, should the tutor get hot if the Hottentot tot hoot and toot at the Hottentot tutor?

The crow flew over the river with a lump of raw liver in his mouth.

She sawed six slick, sleek, slim, slender saplings.

There's blood on the rubber baby buggy bumpers.

HOW'S BUSINESS?

Tailor: "Just sew-sew."

Electrician: "It's pretty light."

Farmer: "Mine is growing."

Refrigerator Salesman: "Not so hot."

Garbage Collector: "It's picking up."

Astronomer: "It's looking up."

Elevator Operator: "It has its ups and downs."

Optician: "It's looking better."

Author: "Mine is all write."

FARM FUNNIES

That new man I hired yesterday doesn't know much about farmin'.

How's that?

He found some milk bottles behind the barn and then came up to me and said he'd found a cow's nest.

Visitor: What do you do with all the fruit that grows around here?

Farmer: Well, we eat what we can — and what we can't, we can!

Farmer: Down on the farm we go to bed with the chickens.
City Feller: Well, in town we'd rather sleep in our own beds.

Sy: What was your peach crop like this year?
Hy: Oh, a big storm blew down half of it — and we'd hardly gathered that when another big wind blew down the rest.
Sy: That's too bad. Could you do anything with the fruit you did pick up?
Hy: Yep. My wife ate one and I ate the other.

That horse you sold me is a fine animal, but I can't get him to hold his head up.
Well, that's because of his pride. He'll hold it up as soon as he's paid for.

Farmer: Where's that mule I told you to take out and have shod?
Hired Hand: Oh, did you say *shod?* I thought you said *shot!*

"We picked a few of your apples," the city motorists told the farmer as they drove away from his orchard. "We figured you wouldn't mind."
"Not at all," shouted the farmer after them. "While you were in the orchard I picked out some of your tools. I figured you wouldn't mind, either."

A farmer was trying desperately to get his mules to move forward, and getting close to losing his temper, when the local minister came by.
"You're just the man I want to see," said the farmer. "Tell me, Reverend, how did Noah ever get these critters into the ark?"

Just back from attending agricultural college, a young student paused to look over a farmer's orchard.

"You know," he said smugly, "your farming methods are really old-fashioned. Why, I'd be willing to bet you don't average ten pounds of apples from each of those trees."

"You'd be right," replied the farmer, snickering. "Them's pear trees!"

Why are you running that steam roller over your field?

Well, I figured I'd raise me some mashed potatoes this year.

A chicken farmer wrote to the Department of Agriculture as follows: "Gentlemen, something is wrong with my chickens. Every morning when I come out of the house I find two or three of them on the ground, cold and stiff, with their feet in the air. Can you please tell me what is the matter?"

In due time, back came a reply: "Dear sir, your chickens are dead."

Farmer: Can you tell me how long cows should be milked?

Prospective Handyman: They should be milked the same as short ones, of course.

"What's that over there?" a small boy wanted to know. He was from the city.

"That?" replied the farmer. "Why, that's a cow."

"And what are those things on its head?" the boy persisted.

"Those are horns," answered the farmer.

Just then the cow mooed.

"Which horn did it blow?" the boy wanted to know.

DAFFYNITIONS

Accordion: An instrument invented by the man who couldn't decide how big the fish was that got away.

Bacteria: The rear of a cafeteria.

Bamboo: An Italian baby.

Blunderbuss: Kissing the wrong girl.

Bread: Used in some restaurants to keep the insides of a sandwich from blowing away. It is also known as "raw toast."

Carbon: A famous opera.

Celery: Rhubarb with sound effects.

Children: Small people who are not permitted to act the way their parents did at that age.

Circle: A round straight line with a hole in the middle.

Cookbook: A stirring volume.

Dancing: The art of pulling your feet away faster than your partner can step on them.

Depth: Height turned upside down.

Divine: What grapes grow on.

Duck: A chicken in snowshoes.

Editor: A literary barber.

Egotist: A person of low taste, more interested in himself than in me.

Embarrassment: When you order something on the menu and find out that the orchestra is playing it.

Fission: A popular sport.

Grudge: A place to keep an automobile.

Home town: Where people wonder how you ever got as far as you did.

Hypochondriac: A person who just can't leave well enough alone.

Jury: Twelve men chosen to vote on which side has the better lawyer.

Nursery: Bawlroom.

Positive: Being mistaken at the top of one's voice.

Public speaking: Diluting a two-minute idea with a two-hour vocabulary.

Punctuality: The best way to avoid meeting people.

Reindeer: A horse with a TV antenna.

Rich man: One who doesn't know his son is in college.

Saddle: A city in Washington state.

Sandwich spread: What people get from eating between meals.

Screen door: Something the kids get a bang out of.

Secret: Something that's hushed about from place to place.

Senator: Half horse and half man.

Skeleton: Some bones with the people scraped off.

Snuff: Stuff that, if you don't feel well, you're not quite up to.

Statistician: A man who draws a mathematically precise line from an unwarranted assumption to a foregone conclusion.

Steam: Water crazy with the heat.

Sweater: A garment worn by a child when its mother feels chilly.

Woman: Someone who reaches for a chair when the telephone rings.

Zephyr: A breeze that got into a travel folder.

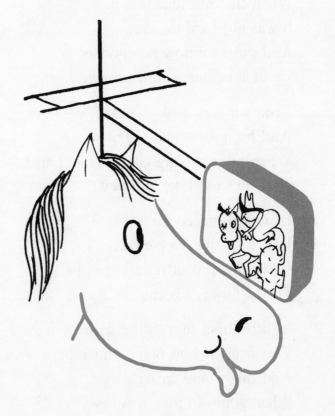

RHYMES WITH AND WITHOUT REASON

'Tis done beneath the mistletoe,
'Tis done beneath the rose,
But the proper place to kiss, you know,
Is just beneath the nose.

Jack be nimble,
Jack be quick,
Jack jump over the candlestick.
Big deal!

Hickory, dickory, dock,
Two mice ran up the clock,
The clock struck one,
But the other one got away.

OLD-FASHIONED FUN

By W. M. Thackeray

When that old joke was new,
It was not hard to joke,
And puns we now pooh-pooh,
Great laughter would provoke.

True wit was seldom heard,
And humor shown by few,
When reign'd King George the Third,
And that old joke was new.

It passed indeed for wit,
Did this achievement rare,
When down your friend would sit,
To steal away his chair.

You brought him to the floor,
You bruised him black and blue,
And this would cause a roar,
When your old joke was new.

If chlorophyll cures every ill,
It is my expectation
That it would pay to run some day
A chlorophylling station.

He rocked the boat,
Did Ezra Shank;
These bubbles mark
O
O
O
O
O
Where Ezra sank.

He went out one lovely night
To call upon a miss,
And when he reached her residence,

                          this.
                    like
              stairs
         up
      ran
He
Her father met him at the door,
He didn't see the miss.
He'll not go there again, though, for
He
    went
       down
           stairs
              like
                 this.

I often pause and wonder
At fate's peculiar ways,
For nearly all our famous men
Were born on holidays.

Women's faults are many,
Men have only two:
Everything they say,
And everything they do.

At railroad crossings,
Here's how to figger:
In case of a tie,
The engine's bigger.

He ate a hot dog sandwich
And rolled his eyes above.
He ate half-a-dozen more,
And died of puppy love.

I eat my peas with honey,
I have done it all my life;
They do taste kind of funny,
But it keeps them on the knife.

"I guess it must be time to go,"
At last remarked the bore;
"A wonderful guess," she answered.
"Why didn't you guess before?"

"I love the ground you walk on."
This was the tale he told.
For they lived up by the Klondike
And the ground was full of gold!

Into the coop the rooster rolls an ostrich egg;
The hen he faces . . .
"Not to chide or deride, but only to show
What's being done in other places."

I never see my rector's eyes;
He hides their light divine —
For when he prays, he shuts his own,
And when he preaches, mine.

'Twixt optimist and pessimist,
The difference is droll:
The optimist sees the doughnut,
The pessimist sees the hole.

Don't worry if your job is small,
And your rewards are few;
Remember that the mighty oak
Was once a nut like you.

I sneezed a sneeze into the air,
It fell to earth I know not where;
Hard and cold were the looks of those
In whose vicinity I snooze.

LIMERICKS

There was a young fellow named Hall
Who fell in the spring in the fall.
    'Twould have been a sad thing
    If he'd died in the spring,
But he didn't — he died in the fall.

There was a young lady of Crete
Who was exceedingly neat.
    When she got out of bed,
    She stood on her head
To make sure of not soiling her feet.

There was an old person of Leeds,
And simple indeed were his needs.
    Said he, "To save toil,
    Growing things in the soil.
I"ll just eat the packets of seeds."

There was an old man of Peru
Who dreamed he was kissing his shoe.
    He awoke in the night
    In a terrible fright,
And found it was perfectly true!

There was a young man from Japan
Who wrote verse that never would scan.
    When they said, "But the thing
    Doesn't go with swing,"
He said, "Yes, but I always like to get
    as many words into the last line
    as I possibly can."

A very young girl — call her Emma —
Was seized with a terrible tremor.
       She had swallowed a spider
       Which stung her inside her —
Gadzooks, what an awful dilemma!

There was a young lady of Woosester
Who usest to crow like a roosester.
       She usest to climb
       Two trees at a time,
But her sisester usest to boosest her.

There was a young maid of Tralee
Whose knowledge of French was "Oui, oui."
       When they said, "Parlez vous?"
       She replied, "Same to you!"
She was famed for her bright repartee.

There was a young man from the West
Who with a young girl was obsessed.
       So hard did he press her
       To make her say, "Yes, sir!"
That he broke three cigars in his vest.

There was a young lady named Sue
Who saw a strange beast at the zoo.
       When she asked, "Is it old?"
       She was smilingly told,
"It's not an old beast, but a Gnu!"

There was a young man from the city
Who met what he thought was a kitty.
       He gave it a pat,
       And said, "Nice little cat."
And they buried his clothes out of pity.

There was a young man of Devizes
Whose ears were of different sizes.
       The one that was small
       Was of no use at all,
But the other won several prizes.

An epicure dining at Crewe
Found quite a large mouse in his stew.
       Said the waiter, "Don't shout,
       And wave it about,
Or the rest will be wanting one too."

THE KIDDY CORNER

Mother: Junior, there were two pieces of pie in the cupboard this morning and now there is only one. Can you explain that?

Junior: It was so dark I didn't see the other piece, Mommy.

Aunt Martha: And what are you going to give your baby brother for Christmas, Billy?

Billy: I don't know. I gave him the measles last Christmas.

Tommy, why did you put a frog in your little sister's bed?

Because I couldn't catch a mouse.

Mother: Eat your spinach, dear. It will put some color in your cheeks.

Little Boy: But Mom, I don't *want* green cheeks!

Little Andy was given an orange by a lady visitor. "What do you say to the nice lady?" his mother prompted him.

"Peel it," replied Andy.

Little Boy: I would like to buy a puppy. How much do they cost?

Pet Shop Owner: Ten dollars apiece.

Little Boy: Oh, but I want a whole one!

Well, Timmy, how do you like school?

Closed!

Teddy: Mommy, may I have a dime for the man who is crying outside?
Mother: Of course, dear. What is he crying about?
Teddy: "Ice cream — ten cents!"

Mother: Junior, what are you doing?
Junior: I'm feeding the monkeys half my peanuts.
Mother: That's nice.
Junior: Yes — I'm giving them the shells.

Little Richard, who enjoyed watching cowboy shows on TV, came home
    from his first day at school and told his mother, "I've got to bring
    a gun to school tomorrow."
"A gun!" exclaimed his startled mother. "Whatever do you need a gun
    at school for?"
"The teacher," explained Richard, "told us that tomorrow we would all
    learn how to draw."

Well, son, what did you learn in Sunday School today?
We learned all about a cross-eyed bear.
A *what?*
Yes, sir. We learned a song about him — "Gladly, the cross-eyed bear."

(Two-year-old youngster, reciting his sounds): "The dog says bow-wow. The cat says meow-meow. The duck says quack-quack. Mommy says no-no."

Father: Look at all of these bills! Rent, telephone, heating, clothes, food — the costs are going up on all of them! I'd be happy if just one thing went down!

Son: Daddy, here's my report card.

Father: How do you like your new teacher?

Danny: I don't like her at all.

Father: And why not?

Danny: She told me to sit up front for the present — and then she didn't give me the present.

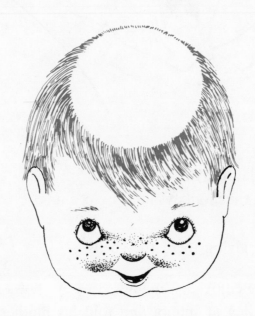

Barber: What kind of a haircut would you like, little boy?

Johnny: One like my father's — with a hole in the middle.

Father: Who was your mother talking to for an hour at the door?

Son: It was Mrs. Harris. She said she didn't have time to come in.

Father: This note from your teacher says that you missed every single question asked of you today. Do you have any explanation?

Son: Yes. None of the questions was in my category.

If I had 12 oranges and gave away 3, how many would I have left?

I don't know — in my class we do arithmetic with apples.

Junior: Mommy, do you remember that beautiful vase that's been handed down in our family for generations?

Mother: Yes, of course.

Junior: Well, this generation just broke it!

"Well, how did you like it?" the small boy's mother asked him as he walked into the house after his first day at school.

"I'm not going back tomorrow," he sighed.

"And why not?" his mother wanted to know.

"Oh," he replied, "it's just no use. I can't read, I can't write — and the teacher won't let me talk."

Mother: Now that you're a Boy Scout, Tommy, what will be your good deed for today?

Tommy: I'm going to teach that girl next door not to stick out her tongue at Boy Scouts!

Father: This report card says that you failed in everything but geography. Can you explain that?

Johnny: Sure. I don't take geography.

Timmy: Let's play school.

Jimmy: All right — but let's play I'm absent.

Mother: Eat your Jello, son.

Little Boy: It isn't dead yet.

May I have another cookie?

Another cookie, what?

Another cookie, please.

Please what?

Please, Mother.

Please, Mother, what?

Please, Mother, dear.

No, dear, you've had six already.

MEDICAL MIRTH

Doctor, every time I drink a cup of coffee I get a sharp pain in my eye. What should I do?

Just take the spoon out of your cup.

A man went to the doctor, his ear torn and bleeding. "I bit myself," he explained.

"That's impossible," the doctor said. "How can anyone bite himself in the ear?"

"I was standing on a chair," the man replied.

Patient: I'm having trouble with my breathing.

Doctor: I see. Well, I can give you something to stop that.

Joe: I suffered from insomnia for years before I went to see this doctor.

Moe: And what did he do for you?

Joe: He told my wife to stop playing the bagpipes in bed.

Doctor: How is your wife getting along on her reducing diet?

Husband: Wonderfully, Doctor. She vanished last night!

Doctor: What do you dream about at night?
Patient: Baseball.
Doctor: Don't you ever dream about anything else? Food, for instance?
Patient: What? And miss my turn at bat?

Patient: Remember when I came to you last year for my rheumatism? You told me to avoid dampness.
Doctor: Oh, yes, of course. And what can I do for you now?
Patient: I'd just like to know if it's all right to take a bath now.

Do you know what to do if a person faints?
Sure — turn him over so his face won't get dirty.

The psychologist was examining his patient.
"How many ears does a cat have?" he began.
"Two," the patient replied.
"And how many eyes does a cat have?"
"Two."
"And how many legs does a cat have?"
"Say, Doc," the patient asked, "haven't you ever seen a cat?"

Stout Lady: I'm putting on too much weight, Doctor. What shall I do?
Doctor: I prescribe regular exercise. Just push yourself away from the table three times a day.

Nurse: Shall we boil the instruments, Doctor?
Doctor: No, let's *fry* them today!

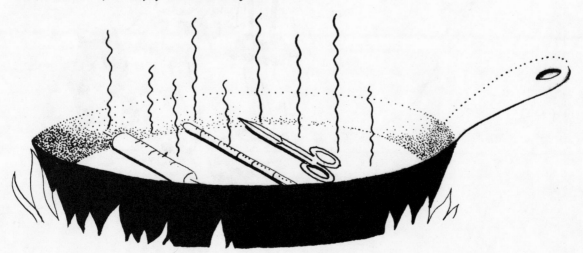

SCHOOL DAYS

Teacher: Billy, you missed school yesterday, didn't you?
Billy: Not a bit!

Student: This isn't fair! I don't think I deserve an absolute ZERO!
Teacher: Neither do I, but it's the lowest mark I can give.

Teacher: Did you write this poem without any help?
Student: I did.
Teacher: Then I'm very pleased to meet you, Lord Tennyson. I thought you had died years ago!

Teacher: What do you expect to be when you get out of school?
Pupil: An old man.

Teacher: George, can you give me Lincoln's Gettysburg Address?
George: No, but he used to live at the White House in Washington.

Teacher: Why don't you answer me?
Willie: I did. I shook my head.
Teacher: You don't expect me to hear it rattle way up here, do you?

Teacher: Give, for one year, the number of tons of coal shipped out of
the United States.
Pupil: 1492 — none.

Teacher: Peter, name two pronouns.
Peter: Who, me?
Teacher: That's correct.

As the first grade's drawing period came to a close, the teacher went about the room to inspect her pupils' art work. At one of the tables, she found Jimmy's picture of a stagecoach, which was lacking in one important feature — it had no wheels.

"Your picture is very well done, so far as it goes," said the teacher encouragingly, "but there are no wheels on the stagecoach. What holds it up?"

The little artist smiled. "Bad guys," he answered knowingly.

The principal gazed sternly at the problem child who had been sent to his office. "This is the fifth time you've been in here this week," he said. "Now, what have you to say for yourself?"

"I'm sure glad it's Friday."

Teacher: Did your father help you with this problem?
Pupil: No, I got it wrong by myself.

I'll never forget the time I went to school. What fun I had that day!
That day? You only went to school for one day?
Why, are you supposed to go back?

(Little boy, saying prayer): God bless Ma and Pa and make Youngstown the capital of Ohio.
Mother: Why?
Little boy: Because that's what I put on my examination paper.

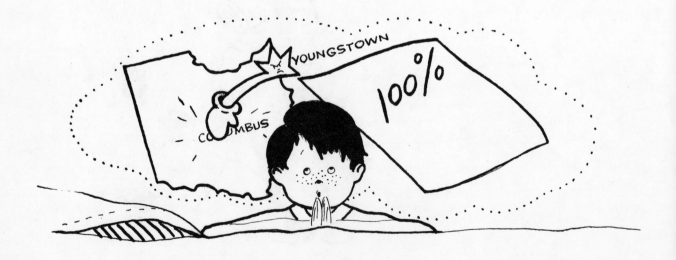

Teacher: Can you tell me where elephants are found?
Willie: Elephants, teacher, are so big they are hardly ever lost.

The teacher told the class to write a composition on baseball. One minute later, little Johnny turned in his written effort. It read, "Game called on account of rain."

The kindergarten teacher looked about the room. All of her charges seemed to be busy at one activity or another — stringing beads, folding and pasting paper, and drawing and coloring pictures — with the exception of one little boy who simply sat in his chair doing nothing.

Coming up to him, the teacher inquired, "Are you free, Harold?"
"No," replied Harold brightly. "I'm five!"

INVENTIONS

I've invented something which will allow people to see through walls.
Wonderful! What are you going to call it?
A window.

I've invented a piano without any keys, strings, pedals or legs.
What would you call that?
Nothing.

What's this peculiar key on your typewriter? I have never seen it on any
    other typewriter before.
It's my own invention. Whenever I can't spell a word, I hit this key and
    it makes a blur.

Once upon a time, a man invented a tonic that could put hair on a billiard
ball. But he died in poverty, because no one wanted to buy a billiard ball with
hair on it.

A cellophane newspaper, so that wives may see their husbands over the
breakfast table.

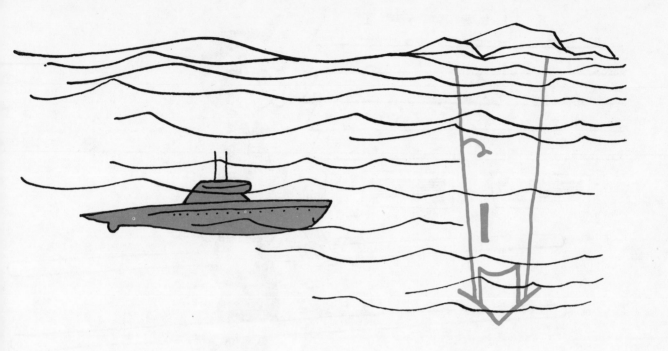

An inverted lighthouse, for submarines.

A pencil with rubber lead, for people who may want to stretch a point.

A cuckoo clock where the cuckoo comes out and asks, "What time is it?"

Neon thumbs for night hitchhikers.

A lamp with no bulbs, for people who like to sit in the dark.

A hollow chisel, for talking through to get a word in edgewise.

An automobile without a horn, for people who don't give a hoot.

A round hole cut in a door, for circular letters.

A perfumed bookmark. If it slips down into the book, just sniff along the edge to find your place.

A shotgun with one barrel on top of the other instead of side by side — for shooting ducks that happen to be riding piggyback.

A stepladder without steps on it, for washing windows in the basement.

A fish hook with a camera on it, to take a picture of the one that got away.

A cookbook full of blank pages, for writing down the names and addresses of good restaurants.

A toaster with knives on its sides that scrape the toast after it pops out.

A car with no wheels. It saves money; just leave it in the garage and ride a bicycle.

Bread with wires in it, for people who have no toaster. All that needs to be done is plug in the bread.

An alarm clock with half a bell on it, for awakening only one of two people who are sleeping in the same room.

DOPEY DOINGS

I saw you pushing your bicycle along the street yesterday.
Yes, I was late for an appointment and didn't have time to get on.

Mopey: How would you like a pair of book ends for Christmas?
Dopey: Oh, that would be fine — I always read the end of the book before the beginning.

Silly No. 1: What do they do with the leftover holes in doughnuts?
Silly No. 2: They tie them up with string and make fish nets.

What time is it?
Five o'clock?
How do you like that? I've been asking people all day what time it is and everybody tells me something different.

Did you sleep well last night?
No, the sheep couldn't jump the fence and they kept landing on me.

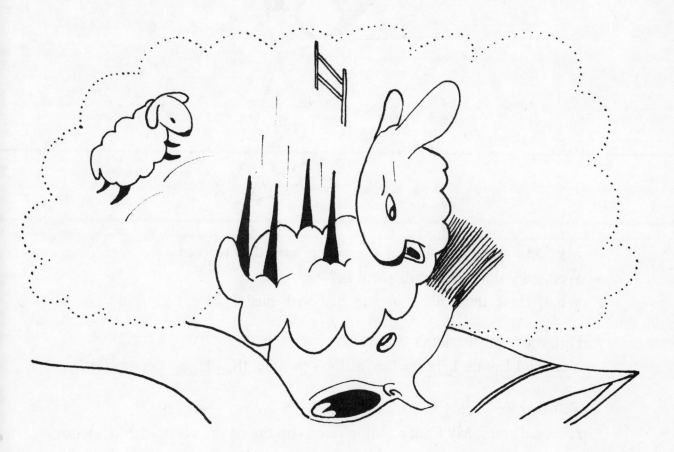

I had to sell my alarm clock last week.
For goodness' sake, why?
It kept going off while I was asleep.

Why do you put your money under the mattress?
So that I'll have something to fall back on.

This match won't light.
What's the matter with it?
I don't know — it lit all right last night.

Billy: If you lost your dog, why don't you put an ad in the paper?
Silly: There's no point in that. My dog can't read!

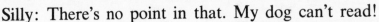

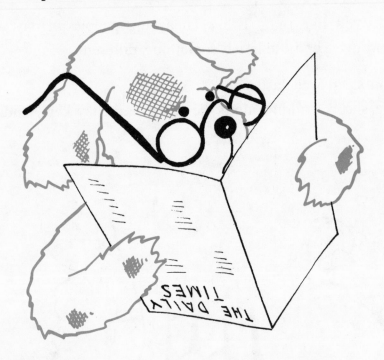

My feet are sticking out of the covers and they're cold!
Well, why don't you pull them in?
What! Have those icy things in bed with me? I should say not!

Did you send the letter air mail?
Yes. And I put a light on the mailbox to show the plane where to land.

Tell me, why are you so half-baked?
It's a sad story. My father couldn't keep up the payments on the incubator.

He was caught cheating in astronomy class.
Really? How?
Well, the teacher asked him to describe the stars and he began hitting
    himself on the head.

Why do you wear that toothbrush in your lapel?
It's my boy friend's class pin — he went to Colgate.

How do you spell Mississippi?
The river or the state?

Did you put new water in the fish bowl?
I didn't have to. The fish haven't drunk what was in it yet.

You look kind of blue. What's the matter with you?
It's just that I forget to breathe every once in a while.

You have your boots on the wrong feet.
Well, they're the only feet I have!

Teacher: Why are you late this morning?
Johnny: I squeezed the toothpaste too hard and it took me half an hour to get it back into the tube.

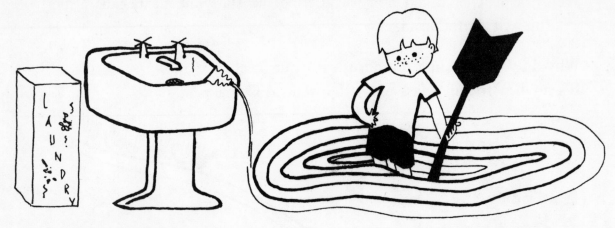

I'd like some DDT, please.
How do you spell it?

Voice on telephone: Is this 1-5-1-5?
Dopey: No, this is fifteen-fifteen.
Voice on telephone: Sorry to have bothered you.
Dopey: Oh, that's all right. I had to answer the phone anyway.

Why don't you answer the phone?
It isn't ringing.
Must you always wait till the last moment?

I'm glad I'm not a bird. I might get hurt.
Why?
I can't fly.

Do you know that I weighed only four pounds when I was born?
Did you live?
You should see me now!

Do you use toothpaste?
Why, no — none of my teeth are loose!

Ow-eee! I just scalded my hand in the hot water.
Why don't you feel the water before you put your hand in it?

First Sportsman: If a flock of birds came into sight and went "Honk, honk!" what would you do?

Second Sportsman: I'd get out of their way.

What are those things floating in the water?

Jellyfish.

What flavor?

Who are you writing to?

Myself.

What does your letter say?

How should I know? I haven't received it yet.

I'm not feeling well today. I ate a dozen oysters last night.

Were they fresh? What did they look like when you opened them?

Oh, do you have to open them?

Do fish perspire?

Naturally. What do you think makes the sea salty?

How do you spell "imbecile?"

I-m-b-e-s-s-e-l-l.

The dictionary spells it i-m-b-e-c-i-l-e.

You didn't ask me how the dictionary spelled it — you asked me how *I* spelled it.

Does your watch tell the time?

No — you have to look at it.

HERE, THERE AND EVERYWHERE

At Albuquerque, New Mexico, a tourist was introduced to an Indian who had a reputation for an astonishing memory. Thinking to test him, the tourist put his first question to the Indian: "What did you have for breakfast on December 16, 1948?"

"Eggs!" replied the Indian, without a moment's hesitation.

The tourist scoffed. "Everyone eats eggs for breakfast," he mumbled. "He's a fraud."

Eight years later the tourist happened to pass through Albuquerque again and he saw the same Indian lounging on the station platform. Jovially, the tourist approached the Indian and said, "How!"

And the Indian promptly answered, "Scrambled!"

An airplane containing the pilot and his only passenger were circling high above a small flying field. Suddenly the pilot cut his motor and began gliding.

"Know what?" chuckled the pilot as he looked down. "I'll bet half of the people down there right now think we're going to crash."

The passenger gulped nervously. "Half of us up here do, too," he said.

A man was once known to be so polite at all times that when he passed a hen on her nest, he tipped his hat and said, "Please don't get up, ma'am."

I suppose you met a lot of Greeks while you were in Athens.
Yes, they have them over there, too.

Tourist: I've come here for the winter.
Californian: Well, you've come to the wrong place. There's no winter here.

What do they call all the little rivers that run into the Nile?
The juveniles.

How do they estimate the population of a Swiss village?
They count the echoes and divide by the number of mountains.

Do you know that Eskimos exist mainly on whale meat and blubber?
Well, you'd cry, too, if you had only whale meat to eat.

Policeman: The signs all say, "Speed limit, 15 miles an hour."
Motorist: But officer, how could I read them when I was going over 50?

The woman who had just gotten on the bus handed the bus driver a brand-new five-dollar bill. "I'm sorry I don't have any dimes for the fare," she said apologetically.

"Don't worry," said the bus driver, reaching for his change-maker. "You'll have fifty of them in a minute."

Is he a worldly man?
I'd say so. He's larger at the equator than at the poles.

A woman walked into a bank and presented a check for cashing.
"Please endorse this," the teller said.
The woman returned a moment later.
The teller looked at the back of the check. It read, "I heartily endorse this."

Postal Clerk: Madam, you've put too much postage on this letter.
Old Lady: Oh, mercy! I hope it won't go too far!

Say, what's the death rate around here?
Same as everywhere, bub — one to a person.

Missionary: Do your people know anything about religion?
Cannibal Chief: We had a taste of it when the last missionary was here.

Customs Inspector: What have you to declare?
Traveler: I declare, I'm glad to get back home.

Wife: There! That does it — the car is parked.
Husband: It's close enough. We can walk to the curb.

Lady of the House: Can you prove that you worked for the Updykes?
Maid: Well, I can show you some spoons with their initials on them.

If a lion were stalking you, what steps would you take?
The longest steps I could!

Mayor: How do you like our city?
Indian Visitor: Very well, thank you. How do you like our country?

A little girl came into a grocery store and said, "My Mommy told me to tell you that we found a dead fly in the raisin bread."

"All right," replied the clerk behind the counter. "Tell you what I'll do — bring me in the fly and I'll give you a raisin."

"Company, atten-shun!" bawled the drill sergeant to the awkward squad. "Lift up your left leg and hold it straight out in front of you."

The squad obeyed the unusual order without question, but by mistake, one rookie held up his right leg, which brought it out side by side with his neighbor's left leg.

"All right, all right," shouted the hard-boiled sergeant. "Who's the wise guy over there holding up *both* legs?"

Lady of the House: Has the canary had its bath?
Maid: Yes, ma'am. You can come in now.

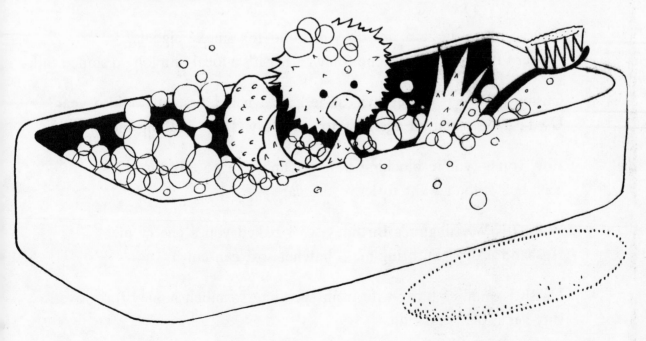

You'd better go a little slower — you're doing 70 miles an hour.
Imagine that! And I only learned how to drive yesterday!

Does your wife know how to park a car?
Well, she doesn't exactly park a car — she abandons it.

Son: Come on, Dad. Buy a new car.
Dad: Wait until I've had a ride in the old one first, will you?

THE LINE IS BUSY

Tourist: How large a fire do you build for smoke signals?
Modern Indian: It all depends on whether it's a local or a long-distance call.

Customer: What makes the car jerk so when I first put it into gear?
Used-car Salesman: Eagerness to get away, sir — nothing more.

Hey, you — you're blocking traffic. Can't you go any faster?
Yes, but I don't want to leave the car.

Wife: It's Washington's Birthday, so I baked you a cherry pie.
Husband: All right, bring me a hatchet so I can cut it.

I wish I could stop my wife from spending so much money for gloves.
Buy her a diamond ring.

Boarder: Does the water always come through the roof like this?
Landlord: No — only when it rains.

Wife: How many times have I told you not to be late for dinner?
Husband: I don't know. I thought you were keeping score.

That's a terrible picture of me. It makes me look as fat as a hippopotamus!
You should have thought of that before you had it taken, dear.

What's the smudge on your face?
Smudge? Oh, well, I just left my wife at the railroad station where I kissed
    her good-by.
But how did you get the smudge?
After I kissed her, I ran up front to kiss the engine!

Mr. Penny (to butler): Please announce Mr. and Mrs. Penny and daughter.
Butler (loudly): Three cents!

Maid: The oil stove has gone out, ma'am.
Lady of the House: Well, light it again.
Maid: But I can't — it has gone out through the roof!

Wife: I'm going to enter this contest. They're giving wonderful prizes for the best ways of completing a sentence in 25 words or less.

Husband: I'll give you a prize, myself, if you can finish *any* sentence in 25 words or less!

Junior: Shall I mail this letter for you, Mommy?

Mother: No, I wouldn't send a dog out in weather like this. Let your father go out and mail it.

I'm on my way to visit my outlaws.

You mean your in-laws, don't you?

No — outlaws. They're a bunch of bandits.

Could you direct me to the First National Bank?

Yes — for a dollar.

A dollar! Isn't that asking too much?

Not for a bank director.

Eskimo Boy: I would push my dog team a thousand miles through ice and snow just to tell you that I love you.

Eskimo Girl: That's a lot of mush!

Lady of the House: If the master brings home some friends for **dinner,** will you be prepared?
Cook: Yes, ma'am — my bag is already packed.

Did you stay at that hotel very long?
No, just long enough to hear their rates, that's all.

Judge: The charges against you are that you ran over this man, and also speeding.
Motorist: Yes, your Honor — I was hurrying to get over him.

Pardon me, does this train stop at Little Junction?
Yes — just watch me and get off one station before I do.

I once carried a hundred-pound load on my back for a mile.
I'll bet it got heavier with every step, didn't it?
No — it was ice.

Hostess: When you serve my guests tonight, please don't wear any jewelry.
Maid: I haven't anything valuable, ma'am, but thanks for the warning.

Is it bad luck to have a cat follow you?
That depends — are you a man or a mouse?

Day after day, the boy and his dog went to school together.
But one day they were separated.
The dog graduated.

A woman leaving a self-service automatic elevator asked an incoming passenger, "What's that 'pass' button for?" She pointed to a button on the panel inside the car.

"That's so you can go by some floors without stopping," was the reply.

"Oh," said the woman. "I *wondered* how one elevator could pass another!"

Mack: I was once a 90-pound weakling. When I went to the beach a 200-pound bully kicked sand in my face. That did it. I exercised hard every day — and in a little while I, too, weighed 200 pounds.

Jack: Then what happened?

Mack: I went to the beach and a 400-pound bully kicked sand in my face!

When Jimmy's pet canary died, his father supplied an empty cigarette carton for the bird, and with much ceremony buried it in a corner of the garden.

"Daddy, do you think my canary will go to Heaven?" Jimmy asked as they walked back to the house.

"Sure, he will," replied the father reassuringly.

"I was only thinking," murmured Jimmy, "that God might be disappointed when he opens the box and doesn't find any cigarettes in it."

Mrs. Jones: George, wake up — I hear a mouse squeaking.

Mr. Jones: I'll oil it first thing in the morning.

Barber: Sir, would you mind turning the other side of your face toward me?
Customer: Oh, are you through shaving this side?
Barber: No, but I can't stand the sight of blood.

Did you know that Nancy married a janitor?
No. How did it happen?
He just swept her off her feet.

Motorist: Remember that car you sold me two weeks ago?
Used-car Dealer: Yes.
Motorist: Tell me again all you said about it then. I'm getting discouraged.

It will take me a long time to forget you.
About how long?
I beg your pardon — have we met?

Doctor: Are you taking good care of that cold?
Patient: I certainly am. I've had it a full month and it's just as good as new.

Doctor, come at once! Our baby has swallowed a fountain pen!
I'll be right over. What are you doing in the meantime?
Using a pencil.

Lady of the House: Will you call me early in the morning, Nora?

Nora: Certainly, ma'am — just ring me.

Maid (to Lady of the House): While you were gone, ma'am, your little Ambrose swallowed a bug. But don't worry — I had him take some insect powder.

Lady of the House: Kate, did you wash this fish carefully before you baked it?

Kate: Now wouldn't that be silly? What's the use of washing a fish that's lived all its life in water?

Butler: I have grown gray in your service and now I'm dismissed. Is there nothing you can do for me?

Master: Yes, you may take my bottle of hair dye when you go.

Bakery Clerk: Here's a very nice cake — I'm sure you'll like it.

Customer: Umm-m, I don't know. That cake looks as if the mice had been eating it.

Bakery Clerk: Impossible. The cat has been lying on it all night.

The Persian Gulf is the hottest place in the world. Fishes have been seen swimming about with their heads out of the water and the perspiration streaming off their faces.

Housewife: I'm sorry, sir, but my husband and I have made it a policy never to buy anything from door-to-door salesmen.

Salesman: Then I have the very thing for you, ma'am. I'm sure you will not want to be without one of these handsome "No Salesmen" signs.

Mother: Danny's teacher says he ought to have an encyclopedia.
Father: Let him walk to school like I did.

Judge: The last time I saw you, I told you that I didn't want to see
     you here again!
Prisoner: That's what I tried to tell these policemen, your Honor, but
     they wouldn't believe me.

Whenever my wife needs money, she calls me handsome.
Handsome?
Yes — hand some over.

The wealthy Texas oil man was greeted one evening by his young son who
     announced happily, "Daddy, I sold my dog today."
"Sold your dog?" asked the father. "For how much?"
"A thousand dollars."
"Really? Let me see the money."
"Oh, I didn't get any money," replied the son. "I got two five-hundred-dollar
     cats for it."

Can you carry a tune?
Certainly.
Well, carry the one you're whistling out in the back yard and bury it.

Do you run a car?
No, I let the engine do that.

Yes, I once got ten dollars a word.
How was that?
I talked back to the judge.

He: You look good enough to eat.
She: I do eat. Where shall we go?

There was a young lady named Bright
Whose speed was much faster than light.
    She set out one day
    In a relative way,
And returned on the previous night.

Did the doctor treat you yesterday?
No, he charged me ten dollars.

I have a very nice apartment for you.
By the week or by the month?
By the incinerator.

How big is this ice rink?
It seats 2000.

A cheerful old bear at the zoo
Could always find something to do.
    When it bored him, you know,
    To walk to and fro,
He reversed it and walked fro and to.

You drive awfully fast, don't you?
Yes, I hit 70 yesterday.
Did you kill any of them?

I just got a job at the Eagle Laundry.
What do you do there?
Wash eagles, of course!

COURT SHORTS

Judge: Order! Order in the court!

Prisoner: Ham and cheese on rye, please.

Judge: If this trial is interrupted by anyone, that person will be thrown
right out of this courtroom.

Prisoner: Hooray for the judge!

Prosecutor: What were you doing on July 15th at 9 o'clock in the evening?

Prisoner: I was eating a hamburger.

Prosecutor: What were you doing at 9:30?

Prisoner: I was taking bicarbonate of soda.

Prosecutor: Do you expect us to believe that?

Prisoner: You would if you had eaten one of those hamburgers.

Prisoner: All I want is justice!

Judge: I'd like to help you, but all I can give you is ten years.

Woman: Your Honor, the accident was unavoidable. I had to run into
the fence to keep from hitting the cow.

Judge: Was it a Jersey cow?

Woman: I don't know — I didn't see any license plates.

DINNER IS SERVED

Waiter (to man who has just had his seventh bowl of soup): You must be very fond of soup, sir.

Diner: Yes, indeed — or I wouldn't be drinking so much water to get so little.

Didn't anyone ever tell you that it's impolite to read at the table?

Yes.

Well, stop looking so intently at your alphabet soup!

Waiter: Sir, we are famous for snails here.

Diner: I thought so. I've been served by one already.

Diner: Waiter, there's a bit of canvas in my fish.

Waiter: Why not? It's a sailfish.

Diner: Waiter, have you ever been to the zoo?

Waiter: No, sir.

Diner: Well, you ought to go. You'd enjoy seeing the turtles whizzing by.

Diner: Waiter, your thumb is on my steak. Remove it this instant.

Waiter: What, and drop it again?

Diner: I can't eat this stuff — call the manager.

Waiter: It's no use — he won't eat it either.

Waiter: Aren't you the same man who complained last week?
Diner: No — after that meal, I'll never be the same.

There was no spoon with the cup of coffee served the diner. "It's going to be pretty hot to stir this coffee with my finger," said the diner jokingly.

A minute later the waiter reappeared at the table with another cup of coffee. "Maybe this isn't so hot, sir," he said.

Diner: Waiter, your thumb is in my soup.
Waiter: That's all right. It's so used to the heat I hardly noticed it.

Diner: Waiter, I think my soup is cold.
Waiter: Well, make up your mind — this restaurant can't be bothered with rumors.

Feeling hungry and despondent, a man walked into a diner and said to the waitress who came up to take his order, "I would like some stew, if you please — and a few kind words."

The waitress went away for a few minutes and then returned with a plate of stew which she set before the customer.

"That's part of my order, all right," said the man, smiling. "Now, do you have a few kind words?"

"Yes," whispered the waitress, "don't eat the stew!"

Why do you eat in cafeterias?
The doctor said I should take long walks before meals.

Diner: Are you the lad who took my order?
Waiter: Yes, sir.
Diner: Bless me, how you've grown!

Waiter: Our chef made pies long before you were born.
Patron: That's when he must have baked this one.

Waiter: How did you find the steak, sir?
Diner: By accident. I moved the potato aside and there it was.

Diner: I would like some oysters. Don't make them too cold. Not too
       large. Not too young nor too old. And I want them right away.
Waiter: Yes, sir. Do you want them with or without pearls?

Look here, waiter, is this peach or apple pie?
Can't you tell from the taste?
No, I can't.
Well, then, what difference does it make?

Diner: Well, waiter, what's on the menu today?
Waiter: Everything, sir.
Diner: Bring me everything. Have it served at once.
Waiter (shouting to cook): One order of hash!

Diner: Waiter, there's a tack in my doughnut.
Waiter: Why, the ambitious thing! He must have thought it was a tire.

Waiter: George Washington once dined at this very table.
Diner: Is that why you haven't changed the tablecloth since?

Diner: Take back this steak. I've been trying to cut it for ten minutes,
but it's so tough I can't even make a dent in it.
Waiter: I'm sorry, sir, but I can't take it back. You've bent it.

There's something wrong with this chicken a la king.
There can't be — the cookbook says it's perfectly delicious.

Waiter: If you order a fresh egg here, you get the freshest egg in the
world. If you order a good cup of coffee, you get the best cup of coffee
in the world, and . . .
Diner: I believe you. I ordered a small steak.

How long can you use a tea bag?
Indefinitely — as long as you keep using rusty water.

Do you want your eggs turned over?
Yes, turn them over to the Museum of Natural History.

Patron: Waiter, this piece of fish isn't nearly as good as the piece of fish
I had here last week.
Waiter: That's funny — it's off the same fish.

Eating, hey?
No, it's spaghetti.

Customer: What are these pennies doing in my soup?

Waiter: Well, sir, you said you'd stop eating here if there wasn't some change in your meals.

This goulash is terrible.

That's funny. I put a brand new pair of goulashes in it.

Waiter, there's a fly in my soup!

1. That will be ten cents extra, please.
2. I've been looking for him all day.
3. What do you expect with the blue plate — a hummingbird?
4. That's all right — he won't drink much.
5. All right, I'll bring you a fork.
6. Ah, cornered at last!
7. That's strange — what kind of soup is it?
8. Yes, we ran out of turtles.

How do foreign dishes compare with American ones?

Oh, they break just as easily.

With which hand do you eat mashed potatoes?

My right hand.

I always use a fork.

ANIMAL ANTICS

A lion was walking through a jungle one day, feeling mean. The first animal he chanced to meet was a monkey.

"Who is King of the Jungle?" he roared, grabbing the hapless monkey with a powerful paw.

"You are, oh mighty lion," replied the trembling monkey.

The lion released the monkey and then came upon a tiger. "Who is King of the Jungle?" he roared again.

"You are, oh mighty lion," was the tiger's answer.

Then the lion met an elephant, to whom the same question was put: "Who is King of the Jungle?"

Without a word, the elephant grabbed the lion with his trunk, whirled him about, and threw him to the ground.

"Just because you don't know the answer," mumbled the subdued lion as he managed to rise slowly, "is no reason for you to get so rough!"

Animals are smarter than humans. Put fifteen horses in a race and thousands of people go to see it. But put fifteen people in a race and not one horse would go to see it.

Mother Pigeon (to son): "Watch your posture — you're beginning to walk people-toed!"

"How will you have your beef today?" asked the zoo attendant.
"O-O-O — W-O-W — O-O-O!" returned the lion so loudly that the windows shook.
And then the attendant knew that he wanted it *roar*.

Mother and Father Kangaroo were on their way to a picnic one day, but every once in a while Baby Kangaroo kept popping out of his mother's pouch. At length Father Kangaroo became impatient and said to his wife, "Why don't you tuck the little one farther down into your pouch so that he won't keep popping out?"
"It isn't his fault," replied Mother Kangaroo. "It's just that I have hiccups!"

What's your cat's name?
Ben Hur.
How did you happen to call it that?
Well, we called it Ben until it had kittens.

An elephant never forgets — but, after all, what has an elephant got to remember?

A man and his dog sat in a theater, obviously enjoying a movie. When it ended, the dog applauded until his paws were sore.
At this sight, a nearby spectator expressed his amazement. "Most astounding!" he exclaimed.
"Yes, it is," agreed the dog owner. "Rover hated the book, you know!"

Mrs. Greenbottle Fly: How's the new baby?
Mrs. Bluebottle Fly: Very restless. I had to walk the ceiling with him all night!

Tim Turtle: I can't think of what I ought to get my wife for her birthday. Do you have any suggestions?
Tom Turtle: Why not a people-necked sweater?

First Dragon: Am I late for supper?
Second Dragon: Yes — everyone's eaten.

A snake snapped at me.
Snakes don't snap — they coil and strike.
This one was a garter snake.

Barracuda: What's that two-legged thing that just fell into the water?
Shark: I don't know, but I'll bite.

Old Hen: Let me give you some advice
Young Hen: Yes, what is it?
Old Hen: An egg a day keeps the ax away.

A man bought a horse from a farmer one day and was just about to ride off in the wagon to which the horse was hitched up when the farmer spoke up. "I think I should mention this," he said. "That horse you just bought has a very peculiar habit — he likes to sit on eggs."

"He likes to *what?*" asked the man incredulously.

"He likes to sit on eggs," repeated the farmer. "I've tried to break him of the habit, but it's no use. He just takes a notion to sit on eggs whenever he sees any around."

"Well, I need a horse," said the man, "so I guess I'll just have to watch to see that there are no eggs nearby." And he drove away.

It wasn't long before they passed a farm, and as luck would have it, there was a henhouse in plain view, as were also dozens of nice, fresh eggs. Before the man could even become aware of the situation, the horse trotted up to a nestful of white eggs and plumped himself down on it.

The man got out of his wagon and then, only after numerous tuggings and words ranging from coaxings to threats, led the horse out of sight of the eggs. Soon they were going along again as if nothing had happened. But then, just as they came alongside a small brook, the horse suddenly turned without warning, waded into the middle of the stream, and sat down again!

The man became quite angry. Leaving the horse and wagon just as they were in the water, he made his way to the nearest telephone and called up the farmer.

"That horse you sold me — the one who likes to sit on eggs . . ." began the man.

"What about him?" asked the farmer.

"Right now that silly nag is sitting down in the middle of a stream!" said the man.

"Oh, I forgot to tell you," the farmer replied, "he likes to sit on *fish* too!"

There was once a nearsighted snake who fell in love with a rope.

Mother Kangaroo was puzzled. She kept scratching in and out of the pouch where her two little youngsters were. Finally she realized what was happening. She reached into the pouch and pulled out the two little kangaroos. Then she set them on the ground and spanked them both soundly with her tail.

"There!" she said. "That will teach you to eat crackers in bed!"

How can you trail an elephant in the jungle?
By the faint odor of peanuts on its breath.

A guinea pig was talking to another guinea pig in his cage at the research laboratory. "You know," he said, "I think I've got Dr. Benson conditioned."

"Really?" said the second guinea pig. "What makes you think so?"

"Well," said the first guinea pig, "every time I go through the maze and ring the bell he gives me food."

Once upon a time there were two skunks named In and Out.
When In was out, Out was in. When Out was out, In would be in.
One day Out was in and In was out. Mother Skunk, who was in with Out, said, "Out, I want you to go out and bring In in." And in two shakes of a tail, Out did go out and brought In in.

"How did you find In so quickly?" Mother Skunk asked.

"It was easy," said Out. "Instinct!"

COMEDY OF ERRORS

Electrician: Your doorbell doesn't work, lady, because you have a short circuit in the wiring.
Housewife: Well, for goodness' sake, lengthen it!

You're supposed to eat a balanced diet.
That's what this is. Every bean weighs the same.

Do these stairs take you to the third floor?
No, you'll have to walk.

A cowboy walked into the ranch house wearing a large, flashing diamond ring on his finger.
"Is that a real diamond?" his friends asked.
"If it ain't," replied the cowboy, "I've been cheated out of a dollar and a half."

Do you believe in clubs for young people?
Only when kindness fails.

Cowhand: Aren't you putting that saddle on backward, sir?
Dude: That's all you know about it, buster. You don't even know which way I'm going.

A bank teller was given a package of dollar bills with instructions to count them, in order to make sure that there were 100.

He started his check and got as far as 58 in his count. Then he threw the package down. "If it's right this far," he said, "it's probably right all the way."

Why don't you buy Christmas seals?
Oh, I really don't know how I'd feed them!

Landlady (to tenant who has been keeping everyone awake with his piano playing): Hey, don't you know there's an old lady sick upstairs?
Musician: No, but if you'll hum the tune, I can play it by ear.

Don't interrupt me while I'm in conversation.
Oh, I'm sorry — I thought you were only talking.

Remember that piano stool you sold me?
Yes.
Well, I twisted it in all directions, but I can't get a single note out of it.

Passing through a small old-fashioned village one warm summer day, a group of hikers decided to rest a bit.

Just as they were ready to move on again, one man, nearly out of breath, came running up and shouted, "Hey, fellers! I just saw a man building a horse. Come look! He's nailing on the back feet now."

Executive: Get me the toy department.
Secretary: Any particular toy you'd like to speak to?

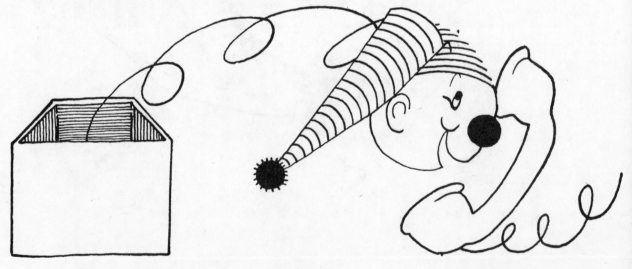

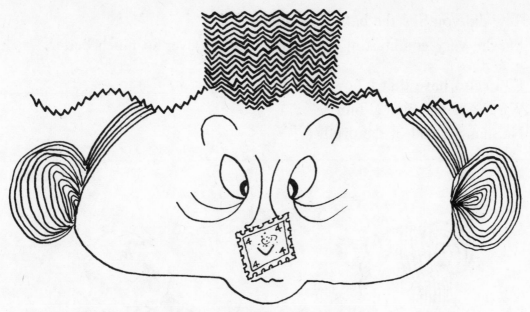

Old Lady: Must I stick the stamp on myself?
Post Office Employee: No, stick it on the envelope.

I just had my appendix removed.
Have a scar?
No, thanks, I don't smoke.

Don't you like music?
I certainly do. I have a zither at home.
Really? I have a brother at home.
No, you don't understand. A zither is a sort of lyre.
Well, my brother is a liar.

Examining a check presented to him for cashing, the bank teller asked the woman who had given it to him, "Can you identify yourself?"

Instantly she opened her purse and pulled out a small mirror. "Yes," she said, after glancing in it for a moment, "it's me all right!"

A man once bought a valuable vase in China. He brought it to his home and there it was an object of admiration and conversation for years. But one day it fell off its pedestal and cracked. And so the man immediately sent it back to the maker in China with orders that it be duplicated exactly.

It took some time. Six years later, he received the vase back — plus a perfect replica, right down to the jagged crack.

How did you like the bath salts, madam?

They're very good-tasting, but a real bath is ever so much better.

I'd like to have that fellow's scalp!

Why? Are you mad at him?

No, mine is full of dandruff.

Landlady: A professor once had this room. He invented an explosive.

New Roomer: Oh! I suppose those spots on the ceiling are the explosive.

Landlady: No, that's the professor!

It's too bad that he always takes the worst possible view of everything.

He's a pessimist, I take it.

No — an amateur photographer.

Do you know that Wally beats his brother up every morning?

How awful!

Yes. He gets up at seven, and his brother gets up at eight.

Fred: I wish I had enough money to buy an elephant.

Ned: Whatever do you want an elephant for?

Fred: I don't. I just wish I had that much money.

Riding Instructor: What kind of saddle do you want — one with a horn or one without?

Dude: Without, I guess. There doesn't seem to be much traffic around here.

How many miles per hour can this boat go?

This boat doesn't go miles — it goes knots.

With all the boats around, *we* had to pick one that goes knots!

Theater manager: Madam, you may not take that dog into the theater — it is not permitted.

Woman: Absurd! What harm could the movies do to a little dog like this?

Do you like codfish balls?

I don't know — I've never been to one.

Jim: I failed my first-aid test in the Boy Scouts.

Tim: Why?

Jim: I tried to bandage a hiccup!

I fell over twenty feet today.

My goodness! Were you hurt?

Oh, no — I was just moving down the aisle on a crowded bus.

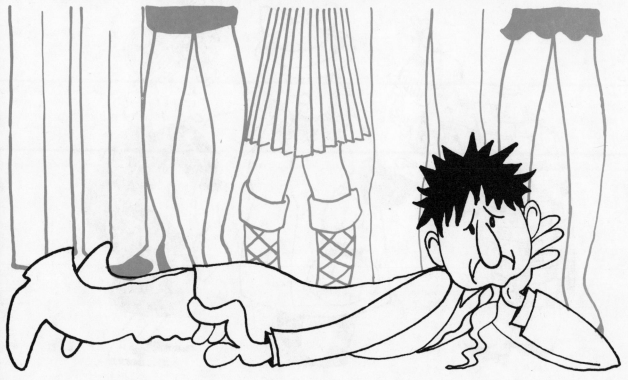

Librarian: Do you want something light or do you prefer the heavier books?
Reader: Oh, it doesn't matter — I have my car outside.

Lovely statue over there. Whose is it?
Oh, it belongs to the city.
No, no — I mean what is it of?
Granite, I guess.
But what does it represent?
About $50,000.
Thanks.

Father: Why were you kept after school today?
Son: I didn't know where the Azores were.
Father: Well, in the future, just remember where you put things.

Chemistry teacher: What can you tell me about nitrates?
Student: Well, I think they're cheaper than day rates.

Three somewhat hard-of-hearing ladies met on the street one day.
"Windy, isn't it?" said one.
"No, it's Thursday," said the second.
"So am I," said the third. "Let's all have a soda."

BONERS

Doctors who examine your eyes are called optimists.

An executive is a man who puts murderers to death.

An autobiography is a history of motor cars.

A psalmist is someone who tells fortunes by reading people's hands.

There are four symptoms of a cold. Two I forgot and the other two are too well-known to mention.

Milton was a blind poet who wrote "Paradise Lost." When his wife died, he wrote "Paradise Regained."

A fjord is a Swedish automobile.

Mr. Koehler came to our schoolroom yesterday and lectured on destructive pests, a large number being present.

An Indian baby is called a caboose.

Lincoln wrote the Gettysburg Address while riding from Washington on an envelope.

The greatest miracle in the Bible was when Joshua told his son to stand still and he obeyed him.

The Golden Rule is: whoever finds gold first keeps it.

Davy Jones was an engineer killed in a train wreck.

A Scotland Yard is something less than three feet.

Gladiators are flowers grown from bulbs.

Poetic license is a license you get so that you can write poetry.

Romans are people who never stayed long in one place.

MARY'S LITTLE LAMB

Mary had a little car,
She drove in manner deft.
But every time she signaled right,
The little car turned left.

Mary had a little lamb,
Given her to keep.
It followed her around until
It died from lack of sleep.

Mary had a little lamb,
It drank some gasoline.
Then it wandered near a fire
And since has not benzine.

Mary had a little lamb,
A little pork, a little jam,
A little egg on toast,
A little potted roast,
A little stew with dumpling white,
A little shad,
An appetite.

Mary had a little lamb,
She put him on the shelf.
And every time he wagged his tail,
He spanked his little self.

Mary had a little lamb,
You've heard it oft before.
And then she passed her plate again
And had a little more.

Mary had a little lamb,
Its fleece was white as snow.
Mary passed the butcher shop,
But the lamb went by too slow.

Mary had a little watch,
She swallowed it — it's gone.
Now everywhere that Mary walks,
"Time marches on!"

Mary had a little lamb,
A lobster and some prunes,
A glass of milk, a piece of pie,
And then some macaroons;
It made the naughty waiters grin
To see her order so,
And when they carried Mary out,
Her face was white as snow.

TALL TALES

There's a girl in the country who has such bright red hair that when she leaves the house before sunrise, the roosters begin to crow.

Snowflakes fall so large in Oregon that parasol makers merely have to stick handles into them.

They are now building ferryboats so long that it takes two captains to command them, one at each end.

There is a pupil in a class who is so thin that when he stands sideways the teacher marks him absent.

There is a farm so big that when young couples go out to milk the cows their grandchildren bring back the milk.

One woman was such a meticulous housewife that she scrubbed the floors of her home until she fell through to the basement.

The fog is sometimes so thick in London that they use it to stuff pillows. By pouring ink on it and chopping it up, it may be sold for coal.

A man once grew so tall he had to climb a ladder to shave himself. And whenever he wanted to put his hands in his trouser pockets, he had to get down on his knees. He could eat nothing but freshly killed meat, else it would spoil before it reached his stomach. As it was, hot soup froze before it got there.

The ducks are so obliging on Long Island that when it comes time to roast them for dinner, they stuff themselves with sage and onions.

There's a fence in Indiana made of pine rails so crooked that every time a pig tries to crawl through it, it comes out on the same side from which it started.

There's one man we've heard tell about who has such a hard name, he spoils a dozen pens in signing one check.

He's so big that when the sun is out, people pay him to lie in his shade.

A photographer once took such a fine picture of a tree that it put forth leaves and bore fruit.

There's a lake in Minnesota that's so clear, you can look down into it and see them making tea in China.

A watchmaker has managed to make some of his watches go so fast they get 14 days in a week.

A thin man had to give up playing "Fetch the stick" with his dog. More often than not, the dog brought *him* back!

His eyes are so large that when he winks, the wind from his eyelids blows out a burning match.

One man devised an original way of fishing in winter. He would cut a hole in the ice that covered a lake, hold a watch over the hole, and when the fish came up to see what time it was, he'd hit them over the head with a club.

An artist once painted a picture of a cannon so realistically that when he finished it, it went off with a boom.

He has such a good temper that he hires himself out in summer to keep other people cool.

There are such tall trees in some parts of Wisconsin that it takes two men and a boy to look to the top of them. One looks until he gets tired, and another commences where he left off.

A barber is reported to have three razors, each sharper than the other. The first razor is so sharp that it cuts by itself. The second has to be held back. And the third cuts about a quarter of an inch before the edge.

One man has managed to live so quickly that he is now older than his father.

MATTER OF OPINION

Marge: Gosh, Mabel, what have you done to your hair? It looks like a wig!
Mabel: It *is* a wig!
Marge: Goodness, you'd never know it!

How did you enjoy the movie?
It was simply awful. I could hardly sit through it a second time.

What did you think of the new play that opened last night?
Very refreshing — I felt like a new man when I woke up.

Tourist: Is it true that an alligator won't harm you if you carry a torch?
Guide: It depends on how fast you carry it, I reckon.

Never put off till tomorrow what you can put off for good.

What must a girl do to have soft hands?
Nothing!

Mary: Peanuts are fattening.
Cary: How do you know?
Mary: Did you ever see a skinny elephant?

TALENTS

You seem to think I can't do a thing.
Not at all. You have more talent to the square head than anybody I know.

I'm studying to be a barber.
Will it take long?
No, I'm learning all the short cuts.

Client: I'll give you $100 to do my worrying for me.
Lawyer: Fine. Where's the hundred?
Client: That will be your first worry.

When you're an actor, you have to be able to turn your personality on
    and off like a faucet.
You must have a leaky washer — all I hear is a drip.

Did you notice how her voice filled the hall?
Yes, I noticed that a lot of people left to make room for it.

Visitor: What a glorious painting! I wish I could take those colors home!
Artist: You will — you're sitting on my palette.

My music is for the ages!
Yes — ages 5 to 10.

I have the leading part at the Town Theater.
Star of the show?
No, head usher.

I was a struggling writer once.
Did you sell anything?
Yes — my watch and my overcoat.

Plumber: I'm sorry I'm late, but I just couldn't get here any sooner.
Householder: Well, time hasn't been wasted. While we were waiting for
    you, I taught my wife how to swim.

Lawyer: As your attorney, I'm sorry I couldn't do any more for you.
Prisoner: Thanks. Ten years was plenty.

Visitor: What does that painting represent?
Artist: That is a cow grazing.
Visitor: Where is the grass?
Artist: The cow has eaten it.
Visitor: But where is the cow?
Artist: You don't suppose she'd be fool enough to stay there after she'd
    eaten all the grass, do you?

Oh, I'm a good speaker. Why, I once spoke to thousands of people at
    Madison Square Garden.
What did you say?
"Peanuts, popcorn, cigarettes, candy . . ."

Sherlock Holmes, the great detective, was sitting in his study smoking his pipe and reading a book. There was a knock on the door, and his trusty friend and assistant, Dr. Watson, entered.

"Good day, Watson," said the great detective. "Don't you think it is a bit warm to be wearing your red flannel underwear?"

"What a magnificent bit of detection and deduction, Holmes!" exclaimed Watson. "But how on earth did you figure out that I am still wearing my red flannel underwear?"

"Elementary, my dear Watson," said Holmes. "You've neglected to put your trousers on!"

Woman on telephone: "Hello, Missing Persons Bureau? I'd like to make a report. My husband disappeared six days ago, and I haven't heard a word from him."

Officer: "Yes, ma'am. If you will kindly give me a complete description of your husband, we will put it on the teletype and send out a seven-state alarm at once."

Woman: "Well, he's very short, quite fat, and bowlegged. He's completely bald and he dresses very sloppily. He has false teeth that don't fit very well . . . Officer, perhaps I'd better forget the whole thing, and not bother with the missing person alarm at all."

SON: "Dad, what's an ocelot?"
FATHER: "It's Sir Ocelot, son, and he was one of King Arthur's Knights of the Round Table."
SON: "Dad, what's algebra?"
FATHER: "It's the language the people speak in Algeria, son."
SON: "Dad, what do they call people who live in Paris, France?"
FATHER: "Parasites, son."
SON: "Dad, you don't mind me asking you all these questions, do you?"
FATHER: "Of course not, son. How else can you ever become educated?"

A visitor to the farm was asking all kinds of questions about the animals he saw.

"Why doesn't that cow have horns?" he inquired of the farmer.

"Well," drawled the farmer, "cows don't have horns for many reasons. Some have them removed, some kinds of cows never grow them, and some get them when they are old. That particular cow doesn't have them," he added, "because he's a horse!"

The teacher was conducting a class in American History, when she called on Johnny Smith.

"Johnny Smith, give me the name of one person who signed the Declaration of Independence," she said.

"I didn't do it, teacher," said Johnny.

"Just for that fresh remark, I want your mother to come and see me after school tomorrow," said the teacher.

The next afternoon, Mrs. Smith came to the classroom. Johnny had evidently told her of his problem.

She strode up to the teacher's desk and glared at her.

"Look, Mrs. Teacher!" she said. "My Johnny is a good, honest boy. Believe me, if he says he didn't do it, he didn't do it!"

A tramp was walking along the road when he chanced to pass a cemetery. Looking across the tombstones, he saw a lovely white marble mausoleum standing in the distance.

"Boy!" he said. "Those rich people sure know how to live!"

LIMERICKS

A fancy young dandy of Shoreham
Had pants made too tight, but he wore
　'em.
He looked very neat
Till he bent in the street
To pick up a dime — then he tore 'em.

There once was a dog named Saggy
Who was both tremendous and shaggy.
He was quite fierce and grim
On the front end of him,
But his back end was friendly and
    waggy.

The poor benighted Hindoo!
He does the best he kindoo.
He sticks to caste
From first to last.
For clothes, he makes his skindoo.

There was a young lady from Crete,
Who was so exceedingly neat,
When she got out of bed,
She stood on her head,
To keep from soiling her feet.

A rocket set out on a flight,
At a speed much faster than light.
It left one day
In a relative way,
And returned on the previous night.

A silly young lady named Stella,
Fell in love with a bow-legged fella.
When the loving chap
Let her sit on his lap,
She fell right through to the cella.

Sam had a big ugly scarecrow on the front lawn in front of his house. It was an eyesore in the neighborhood, and one day his next-door neighbor decided to complain.

"Say, Sam," said the neighbor, "that scarecrow is pretty ugly. Why on earth do you keep it in the front yard?"

"To scare the giraffes away," said Sam.

"That's silly!" said the neighbor. "I've never seen a giraffe around here."

"See!" said Sam. "It works!"

"Pardon me," asked the passenger of the conductor on the railroad train, "but could you tell me where the town of Fishhook comes?"

"At the end of the line, of course."

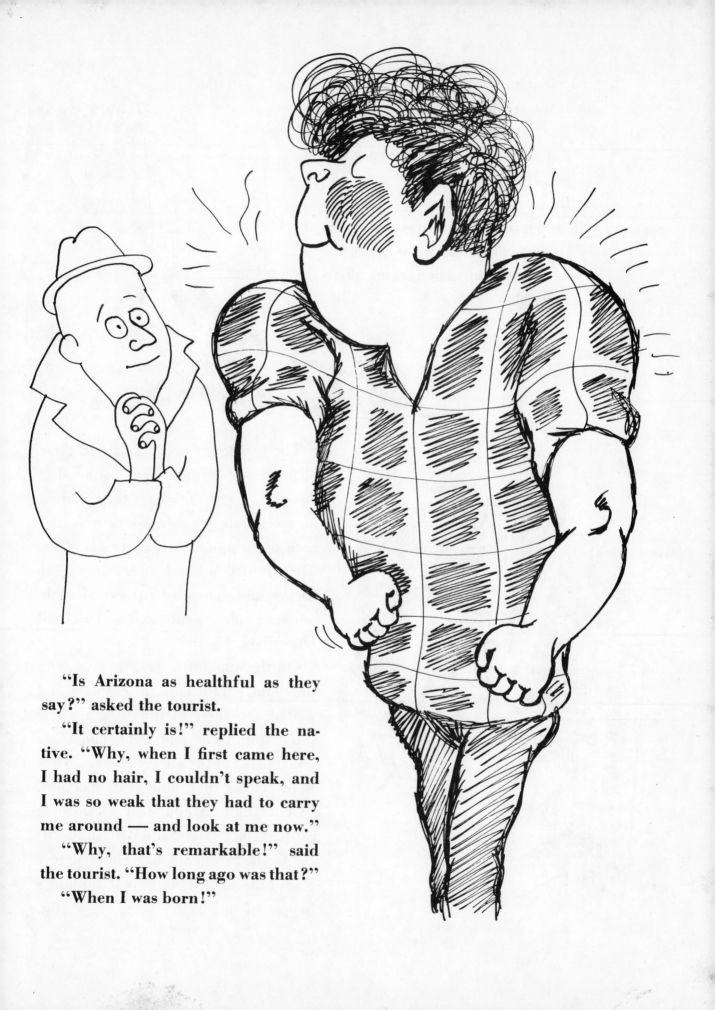

"Is Arizona as healthful as they say?" asked the tourist.

"It certainly is!" replied the native. "Why, when I first came here, I had no hair, I couldn't speak, and I was so weak that they had to carry me around — and look at me now."

"Why, that's remarkable!" said the tourist. "How long ago was that?"

"When I was born!"

A man came into the shoe store and asked the salesman for a pair of shoes one size too small for his feet.

"But why do you want them a size too small?" asked the salesman.

"Because," said the man, "between bills and taxes, and sickness in the family, the only pleasure I have left in life is going home at night and taking off my tight shoes!"

The two secret agents had laid their plans very carefully. They found that the enemy general whom they wanted to assassinate passed a certain corner each morning on the way to his office. They rented a room overlooking the corner and smuggled in several high-powered rifles, a submachine gun, and binoculars.

On the appointed day, they went to the room, got the guns in readiness, and waited for their victim to pass. The usual time came and went, and there was no sign of the enemy general. They were getting more and more nervous.

After half an hour had passed, one of them looked at his watch and said:

"Gosh, he should have been here a long time ago! I hope that nothing's happened to him!"

Little Mabel Moneybags was told by her teacher to write a composition about a poor family. She came up with this classic:

"There once was a very poor family. The mother was poor, the father was poor, and the children were poor. The maid was poor, the governess was poor, the chauffeur was poor, and the butler was poor. They were all frightfully poor!"

As a stout lady was walking down Fifth Avenue with her tiny Pekinese dog on a leash, she passed a big moving van parked at the curb. The driver leaned out and yelled at her:

"Hey, lady, could you lend us your Pekinese dog?"

"My good man," replied the lady, "what on earth could you want with my little Fifi?"

"Well, our truck has broken down," explained the man, "and I thought I might use him to tow us to the garage."

"My little Fifi tow that big truck?" said the woman. "My dear sir, you must be quite mad. He is much too small!"

"That's all right, lady," laughed the man. "We've got whips!"

An airplane pilot discovered that a lady he knew had never been up in a plane, so he offered to take her for a ride. In order to make the ride as thrilling as possible for her, he executed a series of loops and spins.

When they had returned to the field, the lady got out of the cockpit very unsteadily and said:

"I'd like to thank you very much for those two rides."

"Two rides?" asked the pilot. "You must still be dizzy. That was only one ride."

"Oh, no!" said the lady. "It was my *first* ride, and it was my *last* ride!"

LADIES AND GENTLEMEN!
May I present here on the palm of my
   hand,
The greatest trained flea in the world,
PRISCILLA!
PRISCILLA DANCES!
Ta-ta te-um-ta.
Ta-ta te-um-ta.
PRISCILLA SINGS!
Oh solo mio.
Oh solo you-oh.
PRISCILLA DOES SOMERSAULTS!
ZOOOOOOOOM!
ZOOOOOOOOOM!
ZOOOOOOOOOM!
YEA, PRISCILLA!
Clap Clap Clap (applause)
UGH-H-H!
POOR PRISCILLA!

An expert criminologist was applying for a new job in the Police Department. One of the members of the board that was examining him asked whether he had had much experience with lie detectors.

"Experience!" snorted the criminologist. "I've been married to one for fifteen years!"

The policeman brought four boys before the judge.

"They caused a terrific commotion at the zoo, your Honor," he said.

"Boys," said the judge sternly, "I never like to hear reports of juvenile delinquency like this. As I point to each one of you, tell me your name, and what you were doing wrong."

"My name is Tom," said the first boy, "and I threw peanuts into the elephant pen."

"My name is Dick," said the second boy, "and I threw peanuts into the elephant pen."

"My name is Harry," said the third boy, "and I threw peanuts into the elephant pen."

"My name is Peanuts," said the fourth boy.

The owner of a large store was awakened by his phone ringing at one o'clock in the morning.

"I'm sorry to bother you," said a sad voice, "but I'd like to know what time you open the store."

"I open the store at ten o'clock!" said the owner angrily, and he banged down the receiver.

About an hour later, just as the owner had again sunk into a deep sleep, the phone rang again.

"I'm sorry to trouble you any more," said the same sad voice. "But don't you ever open the store earlier?"

"No!" shouted the owner. "I never open the store any earlier than ten o'clock. You will have to wait until then to get in!"

"Oh, I don't want to get in," said the sad voice. "I want to get out!"

Why did the pioneers cross the country in covered wagons?

They didn't want to wait forty years for a train or a hundred years for a plane.

HE: "Aren't you ready yet?"
SHE: "I told you an hour ago that I'd be ready in a few minutes."

An insurance salesman was trying to sell an accident policy to a reluctant prospect.

"Take the case of Mr. Mifoofsky," he said. "Three days after I sold him a policy, he was in an accident and he lost an arm and a leg."

"I know," said the reluctant prospect. "But he was one of the lucky ones!"

The Scotsman was walking along the boardwalk at the seashore with a lady friend.

"Ummm!" she hinted. "Don't those hamburgers smell delicious?"

"Well," he answered, "we can walk back and you can get a better smell at them."

Mrs. Smith was admiring her new vicuña coat.

"Just think," she said to her friend. "The animals that were shorn for this coat lived in South America, the fabric was woven in England, and the coat was finished in New York!"

"What's so remarkable about that?" asked her friend.

"So many people have made a living out of this coat," she replied, "and I haven't even paid for it yet!"

George received an anonymous letter in the mail that read: "You'd better stop stealing my chickens or I'm going to shoot you dead!"

He quickly went to the police station and showed the threatening letter to the officer there.

"Well," laughed the officer, "it seems simple enough. All you have to do is stop stealing those chickens."

"But this letter ain't signed!" protested George. "I don't know whose chickens I'm supposed to stop stealing!"

One day the lion was stalking through the jungle, roaring his mighty roar.

"WHO IS KING OF THE JUNGLE?" he roared.

"You are, oh mighty lion!" chorused the pack of jackals at his heels.

The lion came upon an ape, cowering in his path. The lion lifted his paw, bared his fangs, and roared:

"WHO IS KING OF THE JUNGLE?"

"You are, oh mighty lion!" whimpered the ape.

The lion stalked further, and he came upon a tiger.

"WHO IS KING OF THE JUNGLE?" he asked.

The tiger stood his ground, arched his back, and snarled back at the lion.

With one mighty leap, the lion landed on top of the tiger. He cuffed him with his mighty paw, and held his teeth near the tiger's throat.

"WHO IS KING OF THE JUNGLE?" he growled.

"You are, oh mighty lion," said the tiger, and the lion let him up and he slunk away.

As the lion got to the water hole in the jungle, he met an elephant.

"WHO IS KING OF THE JUNGLE?" roared the lion.

The elephant ignored him, and lumbered on.

"WHO IS KING OF THE JUNGLE?" screamed the lion.

The elephant merely lifted one of his great forelegs and placed it on the lion's back. Then he wrapped his trunk around the lion's body and raised him into the air. Finally, he walked over to the water hole and dropped the lion in.

"You don't have to get so angry," sputtered the lion as he dragged himself out of the water, "just because you don't know the answer to my question."

Mr. Fish, the great chess expert, had a Japanese houseboy who performed all of his duties admirably. The servant, however, did have an annoying habit of interrupting his employer during chess games to ask about the smallest household problems.

Finally, the exasperated Mr. Fish had to lecture the houseboy most severely and threatened to discharge him if he ever interrupted a chess game again.

One day, as a chess game was in progress, the houseboy came into the room and stood there bowing and smiling but not saying anything. After a half-hour, when the game was concluded, Mr. Fish looked up at him approvingly and said:

"All right, Tojo, I see that you have learned your lesson. Now what is it that you wanted?"

"Only desire to inform honorable sir, please," replied the grinning houseboy, "that house is on fire!"

The farmer had a son who went to the city where he opened a shoeshine parlor. Now the farmer makes hay while the son shines.

MOE: "How are you, Joe? I haven't seen you in years!"

JOE: "I just got married."

MOE: "That's wonderful!"

JOE: "No, it isn't. My wife is the ugliest girl in the world."

MOE: "That's terrible!"

JOE: "No, it isn't. She has a hundred million dollars."

MOE: "That's wonderful!"

JOE: "No, it isn't. She squeezes a nickel till the buffalo bellows."

MOE: "That's terrible!"

JOE: "No, it isn't. She owns a beautiful estate in the country with a fifty-room house on it."

MOE: "That's wonderful!"

JOE: "No, it isn't. The house burned down to the ground last night."

MOE: "That's terrible!"

JOE: "No, it isn't. My wife was in it!"

TOURIST (getting ready to dive into the water): "Now you're absolutely certain, aren't you, that there are no crocodiles in this water?"

NATIVE: "Positive, sir — the sharks have scared them all away."

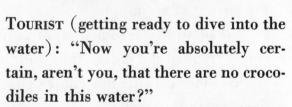

Two Boy Scouts were out on their first overnight hike and found it somewhat difficult snuggling down in their sleeping bags so that the mosquitoes wouldn't get at them. After a while one of them saw some fireflies flying about and he said to his friend:

"We might as well give up, George — those mosquitoes are looking for us with flashlights, now!"

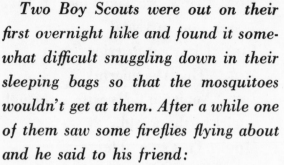

"Your Honor," said the man, "I must have a divorce. I cannot stand to live in the same house with my wife any longer. She keeps a pet pig, and the odor is driving me out of my mind."

"I'll admit that is somewhat of a difficulty," replied the judge, "but couldn't you consider keeping the windows open to get rid of the smell?"

"What!" said the man. "And let all of my pet bats fly out?"

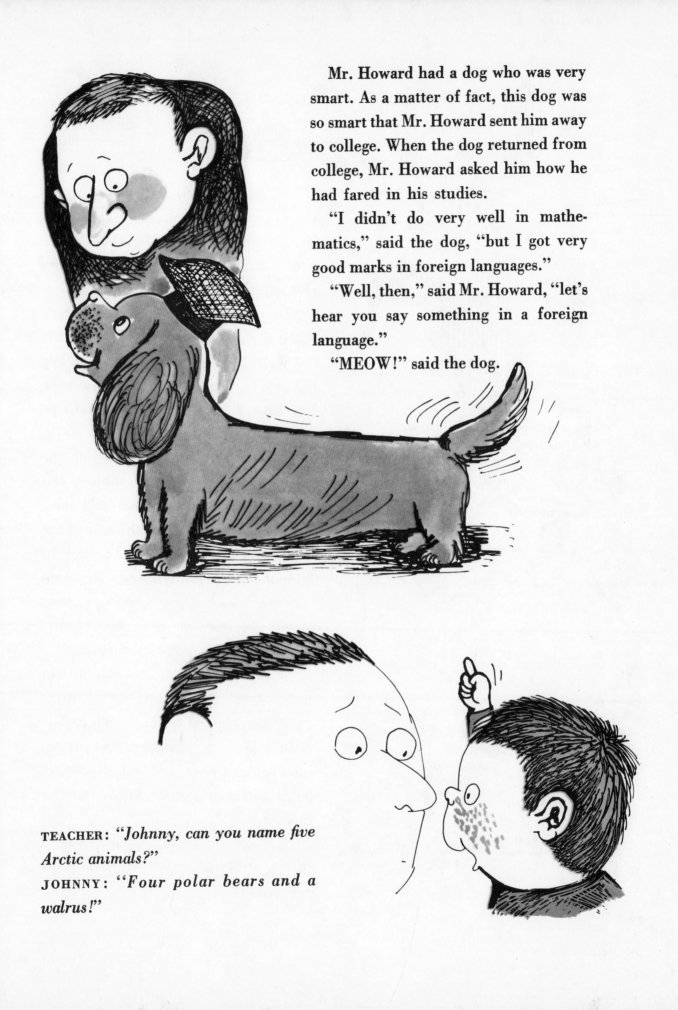

Mr. Howard had a dog who was very smart. As a matter of fact, this dog was so smart that Mr. Howard sent him away to college. When the dog returned from college, Mr. Howard asked him how he had fared in his studies.

"I didn't do very well in mathematics," said the dog, "but I got very good marks in foreign languages."

"Well, then," said Mr. Howard, "let's hear you say something in a foreign language."

"MEOW!" said the dog.

TEACHER: *"Johnny, can you name five Arctic animals?"*
JOHNNY: *"Four polar bears and a walrus!"*

The summer resident walked up to the general store one day. The storekeeper and a few of his cronies were sitting in front of the store, chatting and whittling.

"Do you have any three-inch nails?" asked the summer resident.

"Well, I reckon you might find a keg of them back on the counter," said the storekeeper as he spit some tobacco juice in the ground.

The summer resident went into the store and looked on the counter, but he could find no keg of three-inch nails. Then he looked all over the rest of the store, but he couldn't find a keg of three-inch nails anywhere. He went back outside, but just as he was about to tell the storekeeper of his fruitless search, his eye spotted something.

"Why, look, Zeke," he said to the storekeeper. "That keg you're sitting on — *that's* a keg of three-inch nails!"

Zeke kept on whittling, he spat out some tobacco juice, and he lazily looked down at the side of the keg he was sitting on.

"Reckon you're right," he said. "I guess you'll just have to come back tomorrow!"

Mother Turtle, Father Turtle, and Baby Turtle were sitting down for dinner one night when Mother Turtle discovered that she had forgotten to buy coffee at the store that day.

"I'll go to the store and get it," said Baby Turtle, and he started out.

A little while later, Father Turtle spoke to Mother Turtle.

"Where is that young one? He should be getting back from the store by now!"

"I know," replied Mother Turtle, "I'm beginning to think that he's not very dependable."

Just then a voice floated in from the window:

"If you two don't stop talking about me, I'm not going to go at all!"

A man came running into a drug store and breathlessly said to the pharmacist:

"Quick, I need something to cure hiccups!"

The pharmacist walked around to the front of the counter and slapped the man on the back as hard as he could.

"Why did you do that?" gasped the man.

"Well, you don't have hiccups any more!" replied the pharmacist smugly.

"I never had them," replied the man. "My *wife* has them and I needed something to cure her!"

The little boy wouldn't eat his cereal for breakfast. His mother coaxed, cajoled, begged, implored, threatened, and finally she said:

"All right, if you won't eat your cereal, God will be angry."

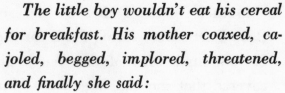

The little boy still refused to eat his cereal, and a few hours later a violent thunderstorm broke out. The sky grew black, the thunderclaps were like bombs falling, and the lightning flashed with an eerie glow.

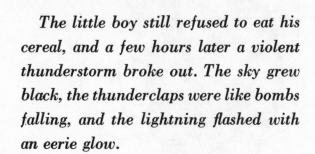

The little boy watched out the window, frightened. Then he said:

"I didn't think God would make such a fuss over a bowl of cereal!"

There's a hole in the middle of the sea.

There's a log in the hole in the middle of the sea.

There's a bump on the log in the hole in the middle of the sea.

There's a frog on the bump on the log in the hole in the middle of the sea.

There's a fly on the frog on the bump on the log in the hole in the middle of the sea.

There's a wing on the fly on the frog on the bump on the log in the hole in the middle of the sea.

There's a flea on the wing of the fly on the frog on the bump on the log in the hole in the middle of the sea.

There's a head on the flea on the wing of the fly on the frog on the bump on the log in the hole in the middle of the sea.

There's an eye in the head on the flea on the wing of the fly on the frog on the bump on the log in the hole in the middle of the sea.

There's a gleam in the eye in the head on the flea on the wing of the fly on the frog on the bump on the log in the hole in the middle of the sea.

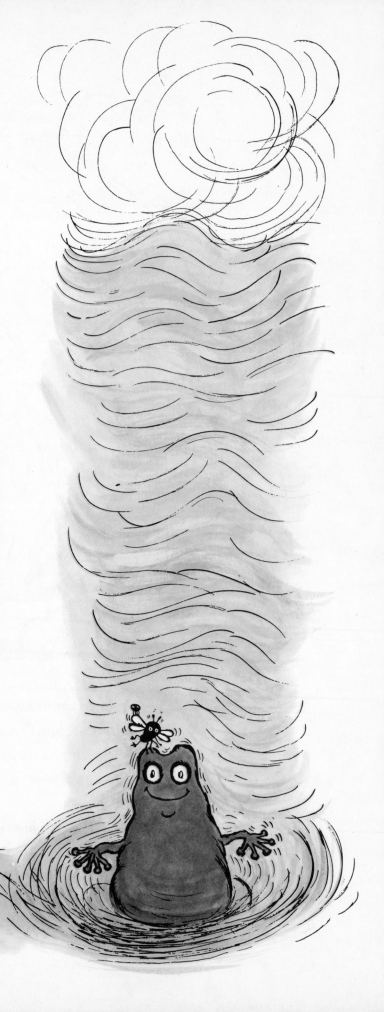

Way down south where the cotton grows,
A mouse stepped on an elephant's toes.
Said the elephant with tears in his eyes,
"Why don't you pick on someone your
   size?"
"Don't throw your weight at me, you
   pill!"
Said the mouse. "Can't you see I've
   been ill?"

KNOCK, KNOCK

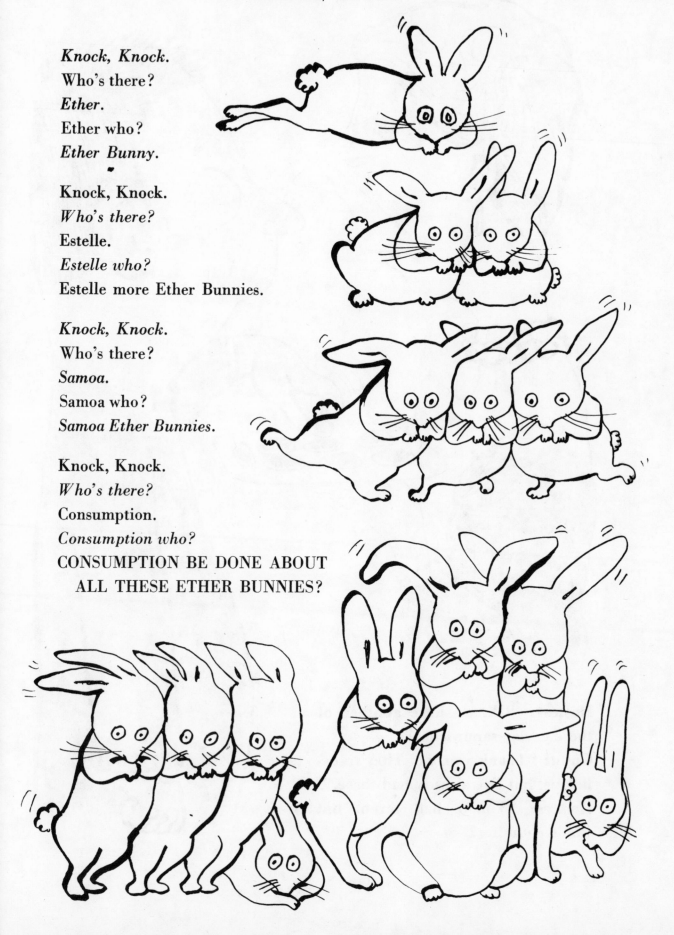

Knock, Knock.
Who's there?
Ether.
Ether who?
Ether Bunny.

Knock, Knock.
Who's there?
Estelle.
Estelle who?
Estelle more Ether Bunnies.

Knock, Knock.
Who's there?
Samoa.
Samoa who?
Samoa Ether Bunnies.

Knock, Knock.
Who's there?
Consumption.
Consumption who?
CONSUMPTION BE DONE ABOUT
    ALL THESE ETHER BUNNIES?

Hostess: "Oh, *do* have another of these caviar sandwiches!"

Guest: "Thank you, no. They're delicious, but I've already had three."

Hostess: "You've had seven, but who's counting?"

MOTHER: "If you were a good father, you would take Junior to the zoo."
FATHER: "I will not. If the zoo wants him, let them come and get him!"

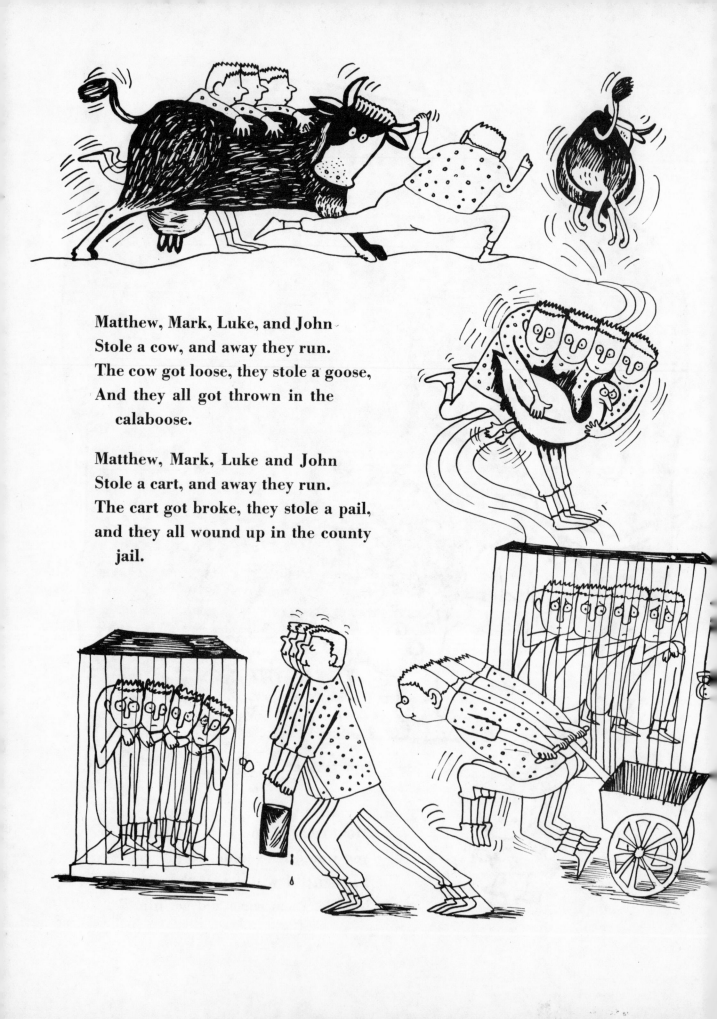

Matthew, Mark, Luke, and John
Stole a cow, and away they run.
The cow got loose, they stole a goose,
And they all got thrown in the
   calaboose.

Matthew, Mark, Luke and John
Stole a cart, and away they run.
The cart got broke, they stole a pail,
and they all wound up in the county
   jail.

SHE: "Darling, I baked two kinds of cake today. Take your pick."

HE: "That probably won't be necessary, dear. My hammer and chisel should be sufficient."

I can't tell you the joke about the dirty window.

Why not?

You wouldn't see through it.

I can't tell you the joke about the roof.

Why not?

It's over your head.

I can't tell you the joke about the memory course.

Why not?

I forgot it.

But I will tell you the joke about the peacock.

How come?

It's a beautiful tale.

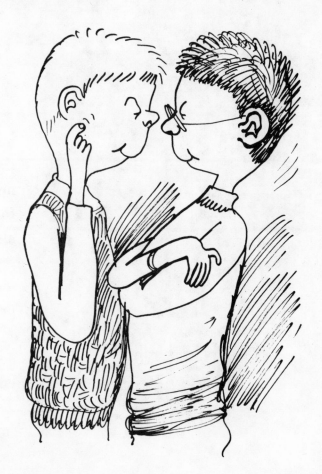

A man and his wife made an agreement that the one who died first would try to contact the other one from the next world. The man passed away before his wife, and she was always on the alert for some manner of spirit message.

One evening as she sat in her living room she became aware of a ghostly presence.

"Darling! Is that you?" she asked.

"Yes," answered the ghostly presence.

"Tell me," she said, "how are things in the next world?"

"Just as lovely as can be," answered the ghostly presence. "Nothing but green rolling hills, a clear blue sky, fleecy white clouds, and clear pure air. And best of all, there is no work to do. All I do is romp and play the whole day through."

"How wonderful!" exclaimed the wife.

"Yes, it is," replied the ghostly presence. "And I have all the green grass to eat that I could ever desire."

"Grass?" asked the wife. "But you never used to like to eat grass!"

"I know," answered the ghostly presence. "But now I'm a bull in Montana!"

A British golfer stepped into a drugstore in America and asked the clerk for something that would be effective against moths. The clerk sold him a box of moth balls. The Britisher returned the next day, then the following one, and a fourth time — each time for another box of moth balls.

The clerk became puzzled as to why he was buying so many, and finally came right out and asked him.

"I say, old man!" replied the Britisher. "You can't expect a chap to hit the little blighters with every shot!"

The same Britisher was walking through the woods with an American friend when they heard a blood-curdling hoot.

"Gor Blimey!" said the Britisher. "What was that?"

"An owl," replied the American.

"Righto, laddie. I know it was an 'owl, but what is doing the 'owling?"

"I've hunted lions and tigers with a rifle," said Hunter Number One.

"I've hunted lions and tigers with a bow and arrow," said Hunter Number Two.

"I've hunted lions and tigers with a club," said Hunter Number Three.

"Good Heavens!" exclaimed the other two. "Weren't you scared?"

"Not at all," replied Hunter Number Three. "There are fifty members in my club!"

Mr. Black was going for his first trip on an airplane, and he was a bit frightened. As the airplane reached two thousand feet, he peeked out of the window.

"Oh, my goodness!" he said, as he looked down at the ground.

When the airplane was up to ten thousand feet, he peeked out of the window again.

"Oh, my gracious!" he said.

When the pilot announced that they were up to twenty thousand feet, he looked out of the window once more.

"Oh, my God!" he exclaimed.

A great voice came back from the clouds:

"YES?"

A man had been having a dream about a beautiful house in the country. Again and again he would dream about the same house, till he felt that he knew it better than his own. What was his surprise one day, as he was driving his car down a strange road, to see the house of his dreams!

With great excitement he drove up to the front of the house and got out of his car. He went up to the front door and rang the bell. A little old lady answered the ring and opened the door.

"Pardon me, ma'am," said the man, "but this house interests me very much. Could you tell me whether it is for sale?"

"It *is* for sale," said the old lady, "but you wouldn't be interested in buying it."

"Why do you say that?" asked the man.

"Because it's haunted," answered the old lady.

"Haunted?" he asked. "By whom?"

"By you!" said the old lady, closing the door in his face.

Two young ladies were whispering and giggling in the movies to the annoyance of a man seated in front of them. Finally, he turned around and said:

"Ladies! Please! I can't hear a word."

"Well, what we're discussing is none of your business!" snapped one.

When a doctor doctors another doctor, does he doctor the doctored doctor the way the doctored doctor wants to be doctored, or does he doctor the doctored doctor the way the doctoring doctor wants to doctor the doctor?

Did you hear about poor Sam?

No, what happened?

He fell out of an airplane.

How awful!

Luckily, he wore a parachute.

Oh, good!

Unluckily, the parachute failed to
open.

Horrors!

Luckily, there was a haystack in the
field below.

How fortunate!

Unluckily, there was a sharp pitchfork sticking up in the haystack.

Terrible!

Luckily, he missed the pitchfork.

Thank goodness!

Unluckily, he also missed the
haystack.

Poor Sam!

Poor Mr. Jones was knocked down and run over by a steam roller. When the ambulance returned him to his house, they found that no one was home.

So the attendants simply slipped Mr. Jones under the door.

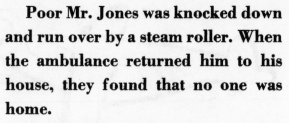

Thaddeus Q. Pinchpenny, the miser, was going over his wife's accounting of her month's expenses.

"Dear," he said, "this extravagance must stop. There is an item of fifty cents for corn plasters, twenty-five cents for aspirin, and three dollars for a tooth extraction.

"That makes three dollars and seventy-five cents that you've squandered on your selfish pleasures!"

In the middle of the show an actor rushed to the front of the stage and shouted, "Is there a doctor in the house?"

A hush fell on the audience, and a man in the tenth row center stood up.

"I am a doctor," he said.

"Hi, Doc," said the actor. "How are you enjoying the show?"

Why is the letter V like a young girl?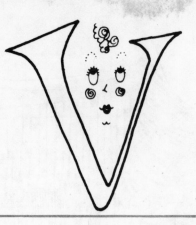

What is taller sitting down than standing up?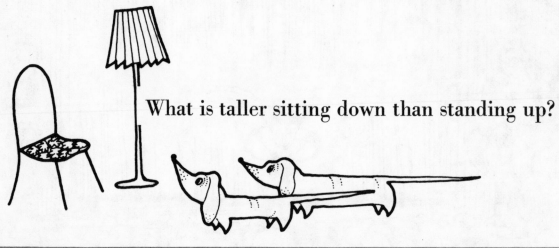

 What can be heard and caught, but never seen?

When can't a frog croak?

**Because
it is
always in love.**

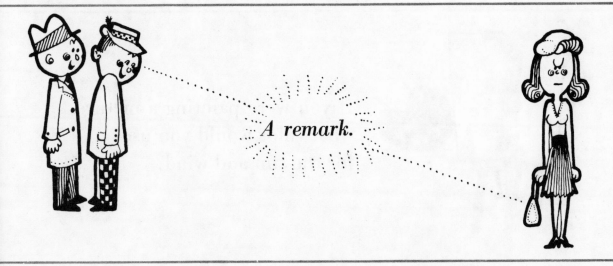

A dog.

A remark.

**When he has a man
in his throat.**

What kind of keys
won't open a door?

What always weighs the same,
no matter what size it is?

If you were painting a picture,
what color would you use
for the sun and wind?

What word
becomes shorter
if you add
two letters to it?

Monkeys, turkeys, and donkeys.

A hole.

The sun rose, the wind blue.

Short.

What did the hen say
when she laid a square egg?

A man smashed a clock
and was brought to trial
for killing time.
He was acquitted. Why?

What question can you
never answer "yes" to?

Where was the
Declaration of Independence
signed?

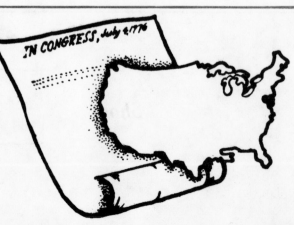

OUCH!

The clock struck first.

"Are you sleeping?"

At the bottom.

What is black and white and red all over?

What animal does a baby
taking a bath resemble?

Why do weeping willows weep?

What can you swallow that
can also swallow you?

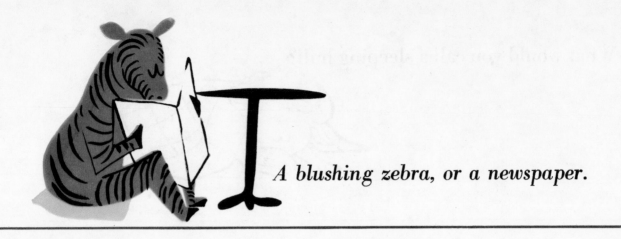

A blushing zebra, or a newspaper.

A little bear.

They are sorry for the pine trees
that pine.

Water.

What would you call a sleeping bull?

What kind of driver
never gets a speeding ticket?

What can you hold without touching it?

What's the best exercise for losing weight?

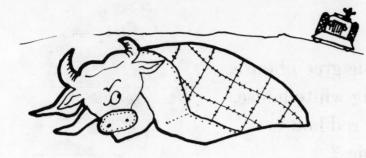

A bulldozer.

A screwdriver.

Your tongue.

Pushing yourself  **away from the table.**

What is the name of a big green house,
That's built around a big white house,
Inside of which is a fine red house,
Full of little brown babies?

Why did the silly billy
tiptoe past the medicine chest?

When is a letter all wet?

What did one chick
say to the other chick
after the hen laid an orange
instead of an egg?

Watermelon.

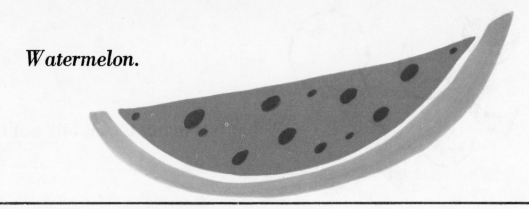

He didn't want to wake
the sleeping pills.

When it has postage due.

"Look at the orange marmalade!"

What has many teeth, but can't eat?

What should you take when you are
run down?

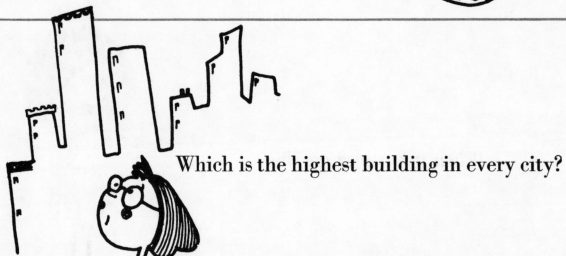

Which is the highest building in every city?

Why did the farmer name one pig "Ink"?

A comb.

The license number of
the car that hit you.

The library always has the most stories.

Because he kept running out of the pen.

If you threw a black stone into the Red Sea, what would happen to it?

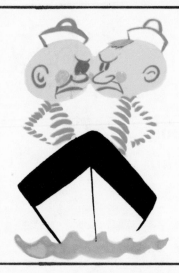

What ship has no captain, but two mates?

When do dachshunds have eight legs?

Why is the letter used in steel mills?

It would get wet.

Courtship.

When there are two of them.

Because it makes MORE out of ore.

What did the mayonnaise say
to the refrigerator?

Which animal is best at spelling?

Why was the silly billy
using a steamroller
on his farm?

For what man does everyone remove his hat?

"Close the door. I'm dressing."

He was trying to raise mashed potatoes.

The barber.

Why is a judge like an Eskimo?

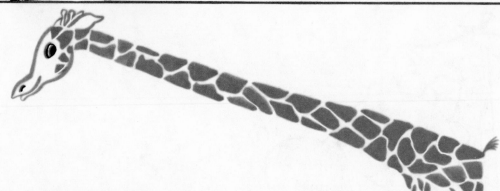

What do giraffes have that no other animal has?

What is the difference between a churchbell and an orange?

What is the last thing you take off when you go to bed?

They are both connected with just-ice.

Baby giraffes.

An orange can be peeled only once.

Your feet from the floor.

What kind of cord is full of knots that cannot be untied?

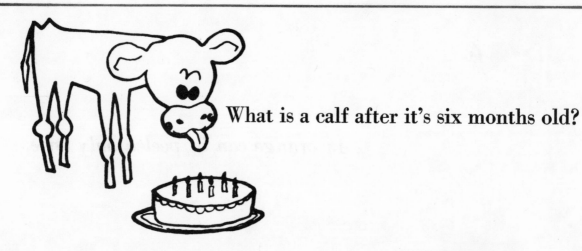

Why is a policeman like a crack in a bench?

What is a calf after it's six months old?

If a car has a horn, but no motor and no wheels, how can it go?

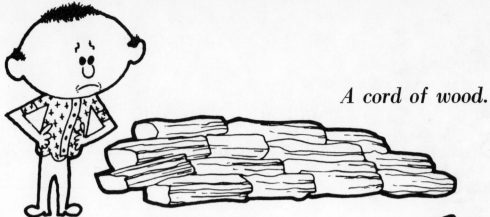

A cord of wood.

*They will both pinch you
if you park wrong.*

Seven months old.

BEEP!
BEEP!

Why did the silly billy
cut a hole in the carpet?

What should an envelope do
when you lick it?

What are most people doing
when it is raining
cats and dogs?

What kind of a bow is impossible to tie?

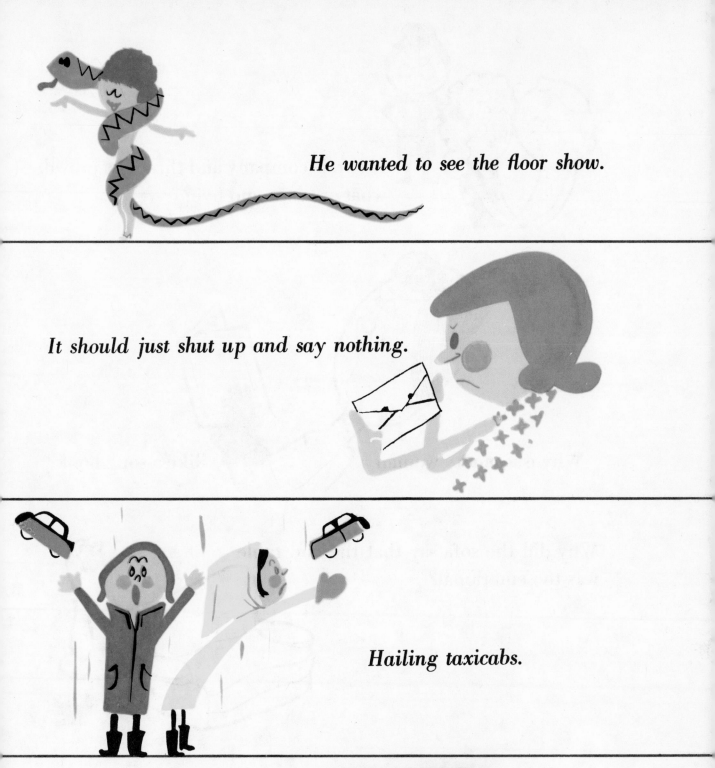

He wanted to see the floor show.

It should just shut up and say nothing.

Hailing taxicabs.

A rainbow.

If two is company and three is a crowd,
what are four and five?

Why is a snooty woman 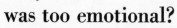 like a song book?

Why did the sofa say that the end table
was too emotional?

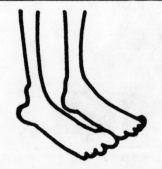

What kind of shoes would you make out of
banana skins?

NINE

They are both full of airs.

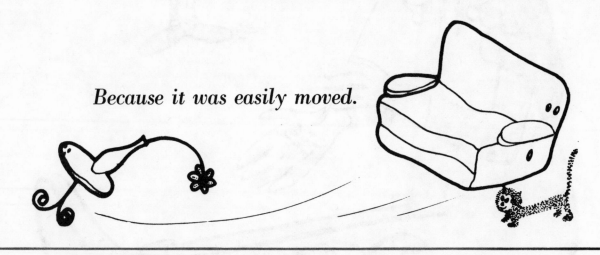

Because it was easily moved.

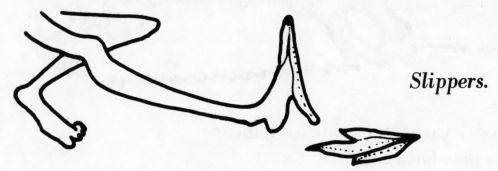

Slippers.

How can you carry water in a sieve?
Freeze it.

What has a thousand needles but does not sew?
A porcupine.

Why does a carpenter value his hands?
Because they have nails.

What is the best way to keep dogs out of the streets?
Put them in a barking lot.

What happens when you feed lemons to a cat?
You get a sour puss.

Why do some babies' hair turn white while they are
    still infants?
Because they have nearsighted mothers who keep
    powdering the wrong end.

When do the leaves begin to turn?
When the teacher announces a test for the next day.

What is the hardest thing in the world to deal with?
An old deck of cards.

Who always whistles while he works?
A traffic policeman.

What happens after a dry spell?
It rains.

How long will an eight-day clock run without winding?
It won't run at all without winding.

What do you have when a bird flies into a lawn mower?
Shredded tweet.

What has a foot on each end and one in the middle?
A yardstick.

What bird is present, but never seen, at every meal?
The swallow.

When are eyes not eyes?
When a sharp wind makes them water.

What must you do before getting off a merry-go-round?
Get on it.

What is green, noisy and
extremely dangerous?
A stampeding herd of pickles.

How high do people usually stand?
Over two feet.

What did the bald man say when he got a comb for a present?
"Thank you very much. I'll never part with it."

What usually happens when there is a big flood?
A river gets too big for its bridges.

When is a dollar like a shirt?
When it's changed.

What is often plowed, but never planted?
Snow.

Why has Santa Claus taken up gardening?
Because he likes to hoe, hoe, hoe!

What comes after a snowstorm?
Snow shovels.

Why does a baby duck walk softly?
Because it can't walk hardly.

Why do weeping willows weep?
Because they're not pine trees. If they were, they would pine.

What is a coquette?
A small Coca-Cola.

Who sells ice cream in Arizona?
Good Yuma men.

What works when it plays, and plays when it works?
A fountain.

What is always behind time?
The back of a clock.

What does "tempest in a teapot" mean?
It means a storm is brewing.

Why did the elephant swallow a mothball?
To keep moths out of his trunk.

What did Paul Revere say after his ride?
"Whoa!"

What makes the Tower of Pisa lean?
It doesn't eat enough.

Why do rabbits have shiny noses?
Because their powder puffs are at the wrong end.

What did the highway say to the road?
"Do you ever get that run-down feeling?"

Why do people laugh up their sleeves?
Because that's where their funnybones are.

What ten-letter word starts with gas?
Automobile.

Which is the most difficult train to catch?
They're all about the same if you let them start first

What do you make when you put two banana peels together?
A pair of slippers.

Why does a sick person lose his sense of touch?
Because he doesn't feel well.

What did the grape say as the elephant stepped on it?
It didn't say a word. It just let out a little wine.

What always works with something in its eye?
A needle.

What happens to ducks when they fly upside-down?
They quack up.

11/5/86

What's the difference between a big hill and a big pill?
One is hard to get up; the other is hard to get down.

What must you do if a dog chews a dictionary?
Take the words right out of his mouth.

What do they call a spy in China?
A Peking Tom.

What goes up and down, yet never touches sky or ground?
A pump handle.

What is black on the inside, white on the outside, and hot?
A wolf in sheep's clothing.

Why did the fly fly?
Because the spider spied 'er.

What lives in winter, dies in summer,
and grows with its roots upward?
An icicle.

Why are some children like flannel?
Because they shrink from washing.

How many monkeys can
    you put into an
    empty barrel?
*One. After that the
    barrel isn't empty.*

Why is winter the best time to buy thermometers?
Because in summer, they are higher.

What did George Washington say to his men before
crossing the Delaware?
"Get in."

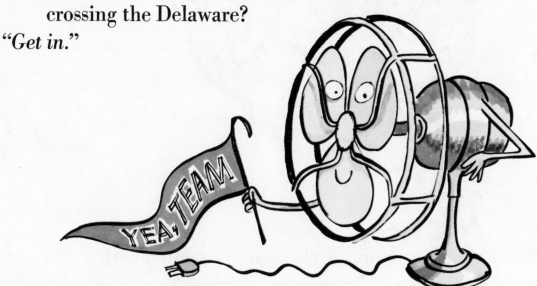

Why is it always cool in sports arenas?
Because there are fans in every seat.

What is the difference between the land and the ocean?
The land is dirty and the ocean is "tidy."

What should you do when you are presented with a marble cake?
Take it for granite.

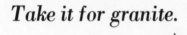
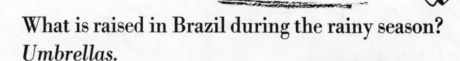

What is raised in Brazil during the rainy season?
Umbrellas.

Why did the cookie cry?
Because its mother had been a wafer so long.

What do animals do when they lose their tails?
They go to a retail store.

Why did the sleepy boy take a hammer to the barn loft?
To hit the hay.

What would happen if you crossed a chicken and a poodle?
The chicken would lay pooched eggs.

If the night has a thousand eyes, what has a thousand ears?
A cornfield.

What is the best thing to take when you're run down?
The license number of the car that hit you.

Who gets paid for never doing a day's work?
A night watchman.

Who took the first taxi ride in American history?
George Washington. He took a hack at the cherry tree.

What is a panther?
A man who makes panth.

What makes opening a piano so difficult?
The keys are on the inside.

When is it correct to serve milk in a saucer?
When you're feeding the cat.

How does the wind blow in the spring?
Easter-ly.

If an athlete gets athlete's foot, what does an astronaut get?
Missile toe.

What is black and white and has fuzz inside?
A police car.

Why is it easier to clean a mirror than a window?
A window must be cleaned on both sides.

The cabbage, the garden hose and the tomato decided to have a race. How did it go?
The cabbage was ahead, the hose was running, and the tomato was trying to catsup.

What day of the year is a command to go forward?
March 4th.

Why do pigs eat so much?
Because they want to make hogs of themselves.

What kind of ants are found in a house?
Occup-ants.

When is a boat affectionate?
When it hugs the shore.

Why do dentists tend to get fat?
Practically everything they touch is filling.

If a man were to take a sledge hammer and smash a clock,
would he be accused of killing time?
Not if the clock struck first.

What starts with E and ends with E and has one letter in it?
An envelope.

When Big Chief Shortcake died, what did his widow say?
"Squaw bury Shortcake."

Why should you never try to sweep out a room?
Because it's too big a job. Just sweep out the dirt and leave the room there.

How do you keep a rhinoceros from charging?
Take away his credit card.

What is a rabbit called who has never
        been outside the house?
An ingrown hare.

How does a clever Boy Scout start a fire with two sticks?
He makes certain that one of them is a match.

What is the best way to keep water from running into
        the house?
Don't pay the water bill.

What does an envelope say when you lick it?
Nothing. It just shuts up.

How can you turn a pumpkin into a squash?
Throw it up in the air. It will come down—SQUASH!

What did one candle say to the other?
"Are you going out tonight?"

When will water stop running downhill?
When it reaches the bottom.

How can you always be two
    jumps ahead of the
    next fellow?
Play checkers with him.

Why does a traffic signal turn red?
You would, too, if you had to change in front of all those people.

Why would George Washington find it hard to throw a silver dollar across a river nowadays?
Money doesn't go as far as it used to.

What did one tonsil say to the other tonsil?
"Better get ready—the doctor is taking us out."